Reflections of a Damaged Child

Acknowledgments

Before I dare acknowledge any inkling of my accomplishments in life, I first acknowledge You God, for it is through Your grace and mercy that I am here today. Thank You for life, thank You for love, thank You for my victories, thank You for my sorrows, thank You for my yesterday's, thank You for my tomorrows, and thank You for everything else that came along the way, because all that I've ever been through made me who I am today . . .

To my mother, Jeri, I love you more than words can express. My love for you is unconditional, just like yours is for me. To my son, **Michael,** I love you more than I've ever loved me. It's with you in mind that I strive to be a better man every day. Let this be living proof that it's never too late to alter your course in life. I believe in you and know that you will live to do great things; it's in our DNA. To **Saniyah**, my beautiful and gifted granddaughter, you are the most amazing young lady in the world. You too are destined for greatness, young Queen, so live your life accordingly. To my brothers **Tracy** and **Choo-Choo** (RIP lil brother), I love y'all. I always have and I always will! Be bigger than your demons and braver than your fears!

I would be remiss if I didn't show some love to my brother **Tyson Amir** (author of ***Black Boy Poems***). Fam, from day one you have been nothing but a solid friend. I appreciate you and all that you represent, bruh. You put the **Black Literary Collective (BLC)** together and the Bay Area community is better off because of it. To my friends, you know who you are. I appreciate everything each and every one of you brought or bring into my life.

And a very special thank you to Poetry. Nothing in my life has ever been as loving and understanding as you. As a confidant you listened to me diligently. As a friend you never betrayed me. As a lover you loved me unconditionally. I appreciate you Poetry, for it is because of you that this beautiful creation called **Reflections of a Damaged Child** ever came to be.

Introduction

Scars

I have a lot of physical scars adorning my skin, physical scars which are the result of an accident or some painful event that happened in my life. When I look at those scars now and think back to how a particular one came to be, I'm unable to mentally recapture the exact sensation of the hurtful feelings I experienced when the damage actually occurred. In essence, my physical scars are simply scabs that healed over a long time ago and then became a distant memory, a vague recollection of a far-flung experience that has no significant relevance on my life today.

On the other hand, I have these mental, emotional, and psychological scars which are incredibly deep; incredibly deep in meaning, incredibly deep in feeling, and incredibly deep in cause and effect. These scars are the result of traumatic childhood events that severely impacted my entire life: instances of sexual abuse by adult strangers when I was five and nine-years old, vicious prolonged physical abuse by a stepfather with a wicked heart and an unforgiving hand that began at age three and went on until I was thirteen. These abuses included my stepfather forcibly placing me behind a refrigerator as a child because I wouldn't stop crying after a brutal beating, or his dangling me over the second floor banister and using that leverage as a threat during one of my parents' fights, and other verbal and emotional abuses from as far back as I can recall. My stepfather's actions took a serious toll on my psyche in ways that made me view myself and the world through a lens muddied with fear and anger that led to a lifetime of self-destructive choices, choices which oftentimes hurt other people.

In March 2010 I discovered I had a gift for writing, a gift that quickly progressed into a passion. Eventually, I developed a profound love for expressing myself through poetry and other forms of prose that was both therapeutic and healing to my spirit. This discovery occurred in the midst of my transformation and self-development as a person. As I delved deeper into understanding why I was the way I was, learning who I am and who I wanted to be, writing played a tremendously instrumental role throughout the entire process. It forced me to peel back the many layers of damage that had been done to me and to dig deep into the scars that grew hard and calloused over time with anger, bitterness, resentment, fear, hurt, and shame. As an adult who came to have a better understanding of self, I was able to venture back into my past, rescue the wounded child within, and help myself heal from the trauma and pain that plagued me for nearly four decades.

Today, rather than use my traumatic experiences as excuses to commit destructive acts, I use my scars as reference points of understanding. I help others deal with and heal from the hurt they are experiencing in their lives, a hurt that has left them scarred and in pain, much the same way mine had once left me.

That's the beauty of writing, it has a healing component to it that can cure our worst ills ...

The following are the reflections of a damaged child ...

Memoir of a Damaged Child

My mother once told me that my stepfather started beating me when I was three years old. I don't remember that far back. But as far back as I do remember, I can still clearly recall the many severe beatings my stepfather administered to me as a child. I vividly remember being a frail, rail-thin five-year-old trying to protect my mother from one of my stepfather's violent outbursts. It's my earliest recollection of his cruel, callous nature.

The Summer of 1974 ...

"Leave her alone! Stop hurting my mama like that!" I screamed at the top of my lungs while grabbing at my stepfather's pant leg. My small hand grasped the rough cotton fabric tightly as I yanked at his clothing, desperately trying to pull him away from my mother.

Smack!

A vicious backhand across my jaw sent me sprawling across the blood-stained linoleum-tiled floor, causing me to violently crash into the kitchen cupboard and hit my head hard against the unrelenting wood. Dazed, hurt, and terrified, I watched in wide-eyed fear as my stepfather forcefully dragged my mother in my direction by her waist-length black hair, taking long-legged steps with an evil expression etched into his facial features.

"Don't you ever put your fuckin' hands on me again stupid ass lil bastard!"

Smack!

Another vicious slap struck me across my jaw. The hot, stinging pain paralyzed me, then I cringed in fear and curled into a fetal position, afraid for my life.

Bap! Bap! Bap!

Repeatedly his booted foot brutally kicked my backside. My screams for help were rewarded with a pitiless punch in the back. Then he grabbed a handful of my afro and snatched me off the floor like a ragdoll.

"If you ever put your hands on me again, I will kill you, do you hear me!?"

Blam!

Before I could respond he hurled me against the refrigerator and refocused his rage-fueled energy on pummeling my mother again.

Maybe that's where he first got the idea, seeing my fragile frame bounce off the refrigerator and knock down the alphabet magnets, causing my childish artwork to fall on top of me. After thoroughly beating on my mother, my stepfather moved the refrigerator with ease until there was a small space between it and the wall. He viciously grabbed a handful of my hair again and forcefully stuffed me behind the refrigerator like an unimportant piece of clothing in some overstuffed luggage. My piercing petition for pity fell on deaf ears.

"This'll teach your lil punk ass about gettin' in grown folks business!" Those were his last words before the refrigerator came to a stop within inches of my face, sealing me off from the rest of the world.

I shivered with bone-chilling fear behind that enormous, immovable object. It felt like I was in a giant coffin. The frightening pitch-black darkness and the petrifying isolation was terribly claustrophobic. For hours I stood on skinny, underdeveloped legs, wedged firmly between a cold hard wall and the black cast-iron grill on the back of the refrigerator. To this day I can still hear the nonstop, maddening, low hum of the refrigerator's motor, mixing with my feeble sobs of defeat; a saddened symphony to my despondent misery. My stepfather made me stay behind that refrigerator for hours, until finally he left the house and my mother freed me from my tormenting captivity.

I felt so unloved! I felt so unprotected! I felt so powerless! I was only five years old!

You would think that it couldn't get any worse, but it did. In fact, it got much worse.

Later that year ...

"No! Nooo! Please daddy, don't drop me! Please don't drop me daddy!" I begged as my stepfather gripped me by my neck and held me over the second-floor banister. My words came out in a hoarse whisper as he choked me with his huge hand.

"Shut the fuck up!" he yelled, and then looked down to the first floor where my mother stood trembling, her tear-filled eyes desperately begging him not to drop me to my death. "Bitch, I will kill this lil bastard if you don't do what I tell you to do when I tell you to do it! Do you understand me!?" Spittle flew from his mouth as he hurled the threatening words at my mother, violently shaking me within his iron grip.

"Please don't hurt my baby, Gerald!" my mother begged as she trembled under my skinny, dangling body. "Please don't hurt him! I'll do whatever you say! Just don't hurt my baby!"

"Get down on your knees then and apologize!" he demanded, forcefully shaking me as he did so. His hand wrapped tighter around my throat; my air supply nearly cut off. I gagged and retched while struggling to breathe. My eyes bulged wide and my scrawny legs swung wildly as I flung my arms about, flailing at his strong, muscular arm in an attempt to loosen his grip.

"I'm sorry Gerald! I'm sorry! I swear I won't threaten to leave again! Please put my baby down! Please put him down!" My mother apologized and begged through sobbing pleas of mercy. A sadistically triumphant smile slowly spread across my stepfather's face as I dangled dangerously from the end of his outstretched arm.

I felt so vulnerable! I felt so helpless! I felt so hopeless! I was only five years old!

Day after day, week after week, month after month, and year after year this cycle of terrorizing abuse continued, worsening as I got older and bigger.

For years my stepfather ruthlessly beat me. For years my stepfather mercilessly verbally abused me. For years my stepfather psychologically tormented me.

His frequent acts of heartless cruelty made me think thoughts no child should ever think. His repeated deeds of brutal callousness made me feel emotions no child should ever be forced to feel. I grew up feeling and thinking I was unloved, unworthy, helpless, weak, hopeless, afraid, neglected, powerless, unwanted, abandoned, targeted, insignificant, undeserving, meaningless, insecure, ashamed, and worthless. As a result, I formed a set of extremely immoral core values that gave life to a very corrupt belief system.

My distrust for people became deeply rooted. Bitterness and resentment eventually followed. Anger bubbled inside of me, ready to erupt and blow up any minute, *every* minute. Hatred toward others and myself festered in my heart for years. Rage resided directly behind so many of those feelings and emotions, ready to rear its ugly head and explode on impulse. I repressed traumatic experiences, thoughts, and feelings as a way of defending myself. In time I learned to suppress the painful thoughts and feelings as a way of coping with the hardships that were attached to them. How else does a child survive?

My mother was constantly under attack during this time period, fending off attacks on her own safety, so establishing a nurturing environment in the home was nonexistent. As a result, I developed incredibly low self-esteem. I had no sense of identity and was taught very little about life and its expectations. As I got older, whenever I went out of the house, I angrily searched for the things I felt were being taken away from my childhood: a voice, a sense of power and control, my identity, and many other needs that were not being met.

They say hurt people hurt people. Well, long before puberty, I unknowingly became intent on proving that theory to be absolutely true!

I began stealing from stores at age six. It was a cry for help. I started breaking into parked cars in our apartment complex and stealing money out of the change compartments at age eight. By the time I was ten, I was throwing rocks at moving cars for the fun of it and breaking into houses stealing whatever I wanted. Fighting had become a common theme for me, especially after my father kicked my ass and encouraged me to go win fights by any means necessary. Aggressive and violent behavior was endorsed, reinforced, and fully supported by my stepfather, the most aggressive and violent person I've ever known. By age twelve I was carrying knives and box cutters to school because they made me feel more powerful and less afraid. Having been beaten by my stepfather so badly for so long, and then bullied by other older kids, at age thirteen I determined that nobody was ever going to hurt me again!!!

The crimes I committed became more and more serious, and I soon found myself in juvenile hall at age thirteen facing armed robbery charges. I was released on probation and then locked up again months later, this time on assault and armed robbery charges. I joined a gang that year because I was looking for something that wasn't present in my household: unconditional love and absolute acceptance. I wanted outright power and the ability to overtly display it whenever I wanted to without any consideration for the consequences. I wanted to be around others who were exactly as I was: deeply damaged children that were severely wounded within. The criminal and gang culture provided me with exactly that.

I felt so valueless! I felt so worthless! I felt so purposeless! I was only thirteen years old!

After running away from every juvenile camp and group home that I was sent to, I was eventually dispatched to the California Youth Authority (CYA) at age fourteen. By then, I was a completely out of control violent child with serious mental, emotional, and behavioral problems. But rather than having my "symptoms" properly diagnosed and treated, I was heavily medicated and sedated with large doses of Thorazine, Haldol, or Mellirell, some of the most powerful sedatives on earth. Whenever I would refuse a dosage, I was physically restrained by staff and forcibly injected with the powerful tranquilizing drug. My hazed hateful mindset only worsened with each traumatizing experience. Rather than sitting me down and figuring out what had happened to me in my past that caused me to regularly act out so aggressively, I'd be wrestled to the ground by half a dozen staff members and forcefully thrown into solitary confinement or a rubber room, total isolation. It was dark, depressing, and claustrophobic in there. In my immature mind, I was back behind that refrigerator, pressed tightly and wedged firmly between a cold hard wall and that black cast-iron grill.

The summer of 1984 ...

"Ungh! Ungh! Ungh! Ungh! Ungh! Ungh! Ungh! Ungh!"

I punched on the hardened rubber walls until I was worn out and exhausted, my fists scraped and bloodied from my relentless assault upon it. The seconds crept by. The minutes merged into hours. I was losing my mind.

"Let me out of here! Please, get me out of here! Heeeeeeelp! Please! I promise I won't do it again!" I pleaded to be freed from my tormenting captivity, only this time my mother wasn't there to move the refrigerator. After hours of fighting my fears and warring with my emotions, I closed my eyes, fell asleep, and got lost in my imagination. I created new worlds in my head and heart that were far away from the one that kept hurting me, much like I learned to do when I was behind that terrifying immovable object with the black cast-iron grill. All the while my hatred, distrust, and resentment toward authority figures grew deeper.

There were times I was stripped out of all my clothing and placed in a cell with no property or bedding for acting out. I would be given one bedsheet after the first day *if I calmed down and complied.* I would be given another bedsheet after the second day *if I remained calm and continued to comply.* After the third day, I would be issued a blanket, and then a pillow, and so on and so forth. This was the state's version of *preventative treatment and rehabilitation.* But to my angry mind, it was just more physical, emotional, and psychological torture. Abuse of another sort by another entity, different authority figures. Everything I thought and felt before these traumatic episodes only worsened after these cruel and unusual state-sanctioned abuses happened.

I felt so mistreated! I felt so violated! I felt so

neglected! I was only fourteen-years-old!

Fast forward a year ...

It was the mid-eighties, and gangbanging was at its most ruthless peak. The Crips and Bloods were engaged in all out warfare up and down the state of California, and so was I. The institutions I was in were little warzones for teenage gangbangers. Fights and riots were commonplace. Impulsive outbursts of corresponding violence were the order of the day.

"Aye cuz, where you from?" a Crip would ask.

"Fool, this Blood! What's up!?" would be my standard response.

Blows got thrown. Mace got sprayed. Cuffs got placed on wrists. And I'd find myself in Administrative Segregation, the hole. Back behind the refrigerator, that terrifying immovable object. Again, I found myself suppressing my feelings and numbing the pain by getting lost in my imagination, my go-to coping mechanism.

"Aye cuz, where you from?" a Crip would ask, again.

"Fool, this Blood! What's up!?" Still my standard response.

Different institutions. Same results. Time after time again. Year after year. Fist fights. Melees. Riots.

Victimizing the victims. Preying on the weak. Enhancing my criminality. It was the evolution of a thug. No counseling took place during this period. No therapy occurred. No rehabilitation came about when it was all said and done.

After serving seven years and seven days, the California Youth Authority released a much worse person than the child who went in. I got out of CYA with aspirations of being the ultimate gangster.

The Fall of 1989 ...

"Aye homie, there go one right there!" I would whisper from the backseat of a slow rolling car with the windows rolled down, finger on trigger, dying to kill someone: someone who reminded me of me, someone who looked like me, dressed like me, talked like me, acted like me.

Pop! Pop! Pop! Pop! Pop! Pop! Pop! Pop!

The sound of automatic gunfire exploded in the night. Hurt people were hurting people. And, unfortunately, I personally hurt too many people.

Within a hundred days I was back in the county jail facing a life sentence in prison. So much damage had been done to me, and because of that damage, I had an overwhelming need to damage myself in every way possible.

When I got my life sentence, I was mad at the world. I went to prison a full-fledged gang member with an "I-don't-give-a-fuck" mentality and a "fuck-the-world" disposition. I was still a criminal who had no desire whatsoever to change anything about myself. As far as I was concerned, *I* wasn't the problem, *everything* and *everybody* else was the problem.

I spent the first ten years of my prison sentence being involved in numerous fist fights and receiving dozens of serious write-ups (rules violations), which resulted in countless trips to solitary confinement; the hole. I constantly found myself back behind that refrigerator, pressed tightly and wedged firmly between the cold hard wall and that black cast-iron grill. I was self-destructing, and I didn't know how to stop it. I didn't even realize I was doing it!

After spending time in the hole with my face shoved in a book, escaping my grim reality by getting lost in somebody's imagination, I would be released back to the mainline. I'd stay out of trouble for a minute, but it wouldn't be long before I pushed that "self-destruct button" again and took flight. Different institutions. Same results. Time after time again. Year after year. Fist fights. Hostile confrontations. Constant drama. Victimizing the victims. Preying on the weak. Becoming the worst person I could possibly be.

A decade into my prison term, while sitting in the hole for "conduct which could lead to force and violence against staff," I had a conversation with myself as I sat in my concrete enclosure looking up at the assault rifle-toting guard in the gun tower through the inch-thick Plexiglas door.

"Damn Mike, you been on this earth for thirty years and you ain't accomplished shit in life!" I stated out loud and reflected as far back as my mind could recall, shaking my head. "Is this what you want for your life, bruh?" I posed the question to myself and responded without hesitation, *"Hell no, this ain't what I want for my life! I deserve better than this! My family deserves a better version of me! The world deserves a better version of me!"* I stated emphatically, disgusted with what had become of my life.

I sat up on my bunk and wrote *"The world deserves a better version of me!"* on a piece of paper and taped it to the wall above the mirror so that I had to look at it every time I faced my reflection. I wanted who I was looking at in the mirror to coincide with what was written on that paper. Day after day I stared at that sign and vigilantly prepared my mind to embrace the challenge that came with it. I became determined to alter my destiny. For the first time in my life I genuinely wanted better for myself, and was serious about making it happen!

Soon after getting out of the hole I stopped smoking cigarettes, a habit I'd developed at age fourteen. There was something empowering about quitting smoking that made me believe I could accomplish bigger and better things, if only I put my mind to it. I took it a step further and stopped gangbanging. I walked away from the gang life, the only lifestyle I'd ever truly identified with. And it was one of the scariest things I ever did. Scary because, for the first time in my life, I was literally and figuratively on my own. It was then that I began discovering little pieces of who I really was and what I really wanted to be in life.

It took thirty years to become the person I had grown to be. And I'd soon find out that it would take me a number of years to become the person that I wanted to be.

At first change came slow for me. A lot of damage had been done, and I had developed a lot of corrupt core beliefs as a result of that damage. I *wanted* to change, but I didn't know *how* to change, so I found myself stumbling and struggling, still reverting back to my old way of thinking and acting at times when faced with adversity. But I was determined to change by any means necessary, so I used every means necessary!!! Reading books, attending self-help groups, doing in-depth introspection, picking wiser people's brains. I slowly but steadily began replacing my old way of thinking with a new way of thinking. I replaced my negative beliefs with positive beliefs. I replaced negative actions with positive actions. I kept working at it and working at it and working at it, until one day I woke up and looked in the mirror and realized I had become a different person.

In 2010, by chance, I discovered that I had a gift for writing. Writing turned out to be a life-changing blessing and a profoundly impactful form of therapy for me. Through writing I was able to explore my deepest issues and put into proper perspective my pain, anger, and all my emotions, thoughts, and feelings. I fearlessly faced my most traumatizing past experiences and overcame my biggest fears, and in doing so, I defeated my most destructive demons. It was therapeutic to be able to reconcile with and rescue my inner-wounded child! I dedicated myself to the process of completely repairing the damaged child within me so I could heal the hurting adult

I'd become.

The Hurt Part

Alone With My Thoughts ...

It wasn't until I was alone with my thoughts
That
It all materialized
And
I finally realized
That
For so long
I had been so wrong
And so gone!
I walked around full of hate
With a rock hard, fragile façade
My middle finger to the world
With a mean-mug mask and an angry-ass nod
My erratic emotions would give way
To the chaotic thoughts festering in my mind
Then,
Mentally,
I'd eventually,
Find myself in places cruel and unkind

Feeling like a young, wild animal violently stalking my cage
Silently suppressing my childish, hostile, savage-like rage
Why was I so mad, I asked?
Why was I so sad, I asked?
Why was I so bad, I asked?
Oh shit!
Then it hit me like a ton of bricks!
The answers hit me relentlessly
Continuously causing me to flash!
As images of a violent childhood full of evil abuses emphatically splash
Across the back of my tightly closed eyelids like a horrific car crash
My Innocence lost, at too young an age
My wholesome young heart, corrupted and filled with an insatiable rage
Tremendously traumatic events caused me to form fucked up feelings unable to assuage
Countless incidences of violent senselessness
Dragged me down a destructive road that was rough, rugged, and unpaved
I was just a child!
I didn't deserve your vile!
I didn't deserve your evil introductions!
I didn't deserve your foul!
Five years-old,
My innocence, maliciously ripped from me!

Only to be brutally terrorized by a wicked and cruel stepfather for years!

My self-worth viciously stripped from me!

Hurt people hurt people!

So, my unfair fuckin' pain was all you sonofabitch's was ever gonna get from me!

Pop! Pop! Pop! Pop! Pop! Pop! Pop! Pop! Pop! Pop!

I shot my hate-filled bullets at the world until the entire clip was empty

I hid my hurt for years!

While I did my dirt for years!

And I did it all like it was nothing

My middle finger stayed on that self-destruct button

But then a light came on and it shined on somethin'

My decency!

My integrity!

My truest, most beautiful inkling of an identity!

That thug ass dude ain't me!

That bad ass bastard ain't who I was born to be!

Hell nah!

This prison life ain't gonna be my legacy!

That's when I looked deep within,

And searched long and hard

As I thoroughly explored who I really am

I cracked that rock-hard, fragile façade that I once proudly and boldly strolled with
Just like an enemy code
I deciphered that confounding shit and I broke it
I stepped up close to the mirror,
Stern-faced and focused
Then I scrutinized my innermost ugly
And took honest inventory of my broken
Just because both of my father's weren't shit
That doesn't mean that I can't be better than the both of them!
So, I reconciled and resolved issues with the damaged child within
And,
Began an incredible transformation that allowed me to ascend
To heights that my wildest imagination couldn't even fathom
God blessed me with gifts that I'm still joyfully unraveling
A good heart
A beautiful mind
And an extremely creative ink pen
And I give Him all the glory
He softened my heart,

Then opened my mind's eye

And allowed me to rewrite my story

But most importantly,

He instilled in me the ability for me to keep it real with me

He gave me the tools to repair my damage and connect all my dented dots

All this,

While I was alone with my thoughts

Reflection

I wrote "Alone With My Thoughts" at a time when I really needed to come to terms with the complex trauma and devastating pain I was forced to endure throughout my entire childhood. I mean, literally, from the second I first breathed in air, I was thrust into an extremely dysfunctional and very volatile world which showed me absolutely no mercy.

In writing "Alone With My Thoughts," I wanted to express how the violent and malicious abuses I suffered at the hands of a wicked stepfather, predatory strangers, and a biological father who never showed up but whose absence, in my eyes, allowed so many of the abuses I suffered to happen in the first place, impacted my entire life. I felt a supremely strong need to shine a light on how damaging the abuses were to me, how deeply they impacted every facet of my life. I also wanted to highlight points that spoke about how I was able to address and overcome those effects of complex childhood trauma.

I titled this poem "Alone With My Thoughts" because so much of my healing, my deeper understanding of self, and the painful process of rescuing my inner-wounded child came while I was by myself, left alone with my thoughts, to contemplate the most painful and damaging events in my life.

Lookin' Out My Window

Lookin' out my window ...
I see so many things that I dislike, some I even hate
For instance, that brotha right there
He chose a life of crime
As opposed to an opportunity to be great
Lookin' out my window ...
I see a damaged child
With eyes full of tears
His mind full of apprehension
While fighting to overcome his fears
Lookin' out my window ...
I see someone suffering
In so much anguish and such turmoil
Good twisted with bad
Not mixing, like water and oil
Lookin out my window ...
I casually observe the obvious reality
A Black Man who is struggling mightily
Trying to overcome a hopeless mentality

Lookin' out my window ...

I see so much potential, and so many beautiful blessings

Or is that just my imagination?

Are those just window dressings?

Lookin' out my window ...

Sometimes I smile at what I see

Because something I just saw

Reminded me of the good in me

Lookin' out my window ...

I see a brighter day

A lot of hope, and greater things ahead

No need to be fearful anymore

But rather hopeful instead

Lookin' out my window ...

At least that's what I thought I was lookin' at

But all the while I was staring in the mirror

And it was only me just lookin' back

Reflection

This was one of my very first poems. I wrote "Lookin' Out My Window" because it's something that I've actually experienced. When looking in the mirror I used to see so many different things about myself, so many things that I didn't like, some things I even hated. But eventually I changed how I saw myself, and that, in turn, changed my mindset for the better, as well as my circumstances.

We all experience feelings of fear, anger, shame, embarrassment, inadequacy, and more, as well as thoughts that sometimes cause us to view ourselves in a negative light when looking out our window (or looking in our mirror). In most cases, as we grow older and experience life, our "perspective" changes, and therefore the way we see ourselves and the world.

This poem was written in hopes of inspiring people to see the best in themselves and not focus so much on their flaws. Too often we get caught up in what "society" says we should be or what we should feel and look like. Other times we grow up making mistakes and poor decisions, and as a result, we feel we are forever flawed because of those mistakes and poor decisions. I believe that people can change for the better much the same way people can change for the worse.

I believe so strongly in that kind of change because I am living proof that something bad can become something good and that what is damaged can be repaired.

The Someone No One Knows

Somewhere in the essence of my existence
The core of me
There lies a quintessential quality
A part of me
A complex conflicted entity that simply wants you
To adore me
But is forever faced with the fear, that if revealed
You'd abhor me
I crave to tell you the truth of me
And not budge
Not brave enough so I live in fear
Of your judge
A slave to the fear of being faced
With your grudge
I long strongly for that unconditional love
Because,
For far too long I never even belonged to a traditional love
And it so hurts
It makes my soul hurt!

Oh, how I long to set my hard down
And fearlessly let my guard down
Reveal my rainbow of emotions and expose to you the truest me
From the blackest, whitest, yellowest, reddest and the bluest me
Divulge my deepest, darkest, most profound secrets
With the hopes that once revealed you'd surely keep 'em
But until that time comes
I'll continue to stylishly wear this lonely suit
And walk this long loveless path in life in these lonely boots
Knowing that,
Somewhere in the essence of my existence
The core of me
There lies a quintessential quality
A part of me
A complex conflicted entity that simply wants you
To adore me
But is forever faced with the fear, that if revealed
You'd abhor me
Sadly, every day that passes older he grows
The someone no one knows

Reflection

This poem is about my fear of meeting that special woman and then struggling with being able to honestly crack myself open and reveal my good, my bad, and my ugly to her. I often wonder if she would be able to deal with my demons and love me unconditionally in spite of my flaws. For many years I was a criminal and a gang member who did a lot of hurtful and destructive stuff. I hurt a lot of people and carry a heavy burden of guilt because of it. I made a lot of poor choices that I wish I hadn't. Sometimes, I wonder if I'll ever find Ms. Right because of all of my wrongs, and I wonder if she'll ever be able to truly love "The Someone No One Knows."

My Conscience Bothered Me

I remember it like it was yesterday

Because to this day

It still profoundly impacts me in many ways

It was a while ago

Sometime back in my early thirties

When my conscience bothered me

And it made me feel so damn dirty

I found myself, literally

While spinning laps around that chaotic prison yard

Wondering around lost, on that penitentiary track

My look and my act hard

Sporting a mean mug mask and a calloused heart scarred

My conscience bothered me,

It pointed a finger at me accusingly

And poked fun at my pride

It provoked the essence of who I am,

A good man

To the point I broke down inside and cried

My chest cavity heaved

As I breathed in past prejudices perceived
And exhaled my angry scorn
My thought process was a rotted one
From a life lived hella wrong
And, in the midst of this storm
I found myself torn
As I struggled with my attempts to free
This new me just born
Who for so long, had been a prisoner to my own forlorn
I was filled with a hatred that I couldn't understand
I had a long talk with myself
And admitted to myself then
That I hated the man that I was
I despised the man that I'd been
At last liberated, I released my untamed tears
Captured and conquered my unchained fears
And it was at that point, that the ignorant man in me died
It was at that point, that the better part of me came alive
It was at that point, that I took control of my purpose-driven life
No longer steered in the wrong direction by a foolish thug's pride
A rotten mind refreshed
My filthy suit undressed

I outfitted myself with a new armor, that was hard-pressed
My complete overhaul
By nearly all,
Was deemed an overall success
Yeah, to get a fuller understanding of it,
You'd have to walk painstakingly slow
Willingly though,
In my dirty shoes
And then stop and squat for a while
And woefully wallow in my muddy blues
In order to feel the angst of my painfully ugly bruise
To better understand why my halo
Used to swing and sway so low
To the point it wrapped around my ankles
And held me hostage to my own hostilities
Keeping me captive like a pair of shackles
But now my halo shines bright
And hovers above my head high
At immeasurable heights
I smile now because,
When so many others quit and gave up on me
Some even hatefully scoffing at me
I believe,
That by a merciful God

This new life was offered to me
And to think, it all began, way back when
He gave me the insight to see
Who I was then,
Who I now am,
And who I had the potential to be
Yeah, it was around then, when
My conscience bothered me

Reflection

A bunch of this poem is self-explanatory, but to give you a better understanding on what it meant to me and why I wrote it, let me break it down for you. I decided to walk away from the gang life when I turned thirty. It wasn't planned or well thought out. I just reached a point in my life where I didn't feel like the thug life was the kind of life I wanted to continue living. I had been a gang member since age thirteen, so all I knew was the gang life. Being locked up, no matter what prison I was in, no matter what yard I was on, there was always another Blood on the yard, and that was something I always identified with, being a Blood.

When I stopped gang banging, I stopped for real. I didn't hang out anymore, and I didn't socialize with the people with whom I had strongly identified with most of my life. By choice, I was forced to stand on my own and walk around the yard by myself. I no longer had a group to cling to, and for a while I felt very alone. It was then that I realized that I had been wearing a thug mask for so long that I had lost my true identity in the process. I truly didn't know who I was! The more I stood on my own and walked alone, the more I got to know the real me, the true me. My conscience made me look deep within until I rediscovered who I truly am. I had to face my ugly. I struggled with right and wrong for a while, but eventually right won out and I committed myself to living my life accordingly.

At the end of the day, people can feel and say what they want to feel and say, but only God can judge you. I try to do the right thing because it's the right thing to do, and I'm willing to live with the consequences of that belief.

When I talk about walking painstakingly slow, willing though, and stopping and squatting for a while to wallow in my muddy blues in order to feel the angst of my painfully ugly bruise, that's my way of saying don't pass judgment on me until you walked in my shoes and experienced my pain. In turn I treat others with that same regard.

When I talk about being a hostage to my hostilities, that's my way of saying I was my own worst enemy, and many of my life scars were self-inflicted wounds. I had to free myself from the bondage of a false identity and phony facade I had long ago adopted. In order for me to become who I was supposed to be, I had to shed that false me I had cloaked myself in when I was a kid.

If your conscience is bothering you, then it's a very good chance that you are not liking some of the things you are doing in your life; you are not proud of who or what you are. If your conscience bothers you, don't be afraid to summon the courage to meet the challenge of changing your circumstances, changing you.

I Love You Bruh ... Take Care ... Goodbye ...

On a bright sunny day in May, 1972
The world was blessed with something beautiful, something special;
The world was blessed with you,
Gerald Morris Jr., known to everyone else as Choo-Choo
Forty-three and a half years later, lil bruh, you gone too soon!
Now I'm frantically chasin' after memories
Of all the good times, days past, seemingly gone.
Priceless thoughts and precious recollections
Eternal in my heart,
Where they will forever reside and live on
I miss you!
We miss you!
Damn it, Choo, I wasn't finished with you!
In this complicated world, you managed to keep it simple
I'll never forget your radiant smile
Or those deep, disarming dimples

The kind words of encouragement that you were always quick to share
Or the countless occasions of comradery that truly showed you cared
Our flashes of a childhood full of laughter
All the unforgettable, joyous times:
Going to the movies
Playing up at the park
And especially riding our bikes
Your temper tantrums
Your stubborn desire to always be right
Man Choo, I even miss our petty fights!
All the years we spent apart
I hope you know that you were always in my heart
I took you everywhere I went
I included you in everything I did
Just like when we were kids
Precious moments in time that will forever be alive in my mind
You weren't just my baby brother
You were always my faithful friend
Choo, you were one-of-a-kind
You were many things to many people, just by being you
You were a real one, a good man with a nomadic spirit

And to your essence you remained true,
Misunderstood at times, but I understood you through and through
You were a teacher; you taught me how to love without condition
You were a rebel; you did you without apology
And you did it on your terms without permission!
You were the truest kind of friend
Literally, you were loyal and loving to the very end
Baby brother, you were flawed, but to me you were flawless
You were wonderful, and you were awesome
And you were all of these things to all of us
Yes, you were many things to many people
But you were *everything* to me
So, with tears in my eyes
And as my heart screams out and cries
I strongly reiterate the last words we shared with each other;
"I love you bruh ... Take care ... Goodbye ..."

Reflection

I wrote this poem in memory of my little brother, who unexpectedly passed away in 2015 at the age of forty-three. I wanted to honor his memory and tell the world about him because he was such a good-hearted person. He deserves to be remembered as such. This was also a way for me to express my pain and all of the other emotions that were smothering my heart and head with his loss. I never cried as much as I cried when my little brother died! Writing this poem was extremely therapeutic for me. It was something that allowed me to navigate through my feelings privately, before I chose to share them publicly. To this day, I break down and have a helluva deep cry anytime I read this poem, or think of my little brother.
I miss Choo-Choo more than I've ever missed anything in my life!!!

This Caged Bird

I've been trapped behind bars for most of my life
Decorated with deep scars that shine vivid with my strife
Once hopeless, I never thought I'd ever be free
So, I did everything I could to self-destruct despicable me
But then God blessed me and revealed to me a beautiful gift
My transformation was rather swift when my spirits were uplifted
He gave me a pen, and the ability to pour out my entire imagination
Written expressions of my truest emotions
Ink painted portraits of how I feel
Often times fantasy and fairytale
But far too often simply my real
I've always heard that the caged bird sings
Never truly understanding exactly what that means
Until my heart and mind were exposed to bigger and better things
It was then, when

I discovered who I was, who I am, and who I am supposed to be
I learned how to fly
Hella high!
When I spread my wings wide
I'm so grown and on my own
This caged bird has flown!
I fly high and ascend skyward toward positive things unknown
These written expressions of my truest emotions
Brilliant bursts of enlightened explosions
Having no clue what my tomorrows may bring
I embrace everything today is giving to me;
The breath of life!
My reason for being!
Creating ink-painted portraits from gifts I was given
Drawing articulate pictures of the tragedy and triumph I live in
Graphically painted tales of pleasure, pain, joy, and suffering
The wonderful delight of a beautiful blessing
And the ugly consequence of a wicked sin
Penning street-lit fiction;
The harshest aspects of gritty street life told

Hot revelations of the urban cold
Intricately woven tales twisting high and low
Thrilling mysteries dramatically exposed
Eloquently sketched visions from what lies behind eyes closed
And poignantly penned poetry of the purest prose
This caged bird not only sings
I'm wide awake while I'm living my dreams!
My body may be captive, but my mind is free!
As I fly high and soar throughout the unexplored
Existing isn't enough, I want so much more!
Written expressions of my truest emotions
Ink painted portraits of what I see
Relishing in the fact that I can pick up a pen and truly be me
Taking pleasure in the idea that I can be anything I choose to be
This caged bird is now flying so beautifully free
I'm flying so beautiful and free!

Reflection

"This Caged Bird" was written as my way of expressing to the world that despite the fact that I was locked up for over three and a half decades, I found my freedom after getting to know myself through much soul-searching and in the process discovering I was blessed with the gift of writing. In "This Caged Bird" I make analogies that equate freedom with writing. I learned early on that writing can be very healing. When I was younger, I learned a lot of things about myself when I read books. I've learned a lot about ME while penning novels. As an author, I've learned so much more about myself when I was forced to look inward in order to reveal the truth about a particular matter. This especially holds true when I was required to dig deep in my emotional archives to further develop certain characters in order to truly bring them to life in a story and make them pop off the page and enter the reader's heart. When you're able to be honest with yourself, and you have a profound desire to be the best you that you can be, then this experience can truly be eye-opening.

I was a caged bird because I was incarcerated, but even before that I was a caged bird because I was living in a mental prison that I'd built to protect myself from the complex trauma I was constantly experiencing. Knowledge of self, combined with the ability to write with a certain level of emotional intelligence, freed me from the mental and psychological bondage I had put myself in when I was a terrified child under constant physical and psychological attack.

In closing, with this reflection, I would like to pay homage to the late great Maya Angelo, from whom I first heard the phrase "Why the Caged Bird Sings," one of the most beautiful poems ever written.

Freedom to Me

Freedom to me
Was unbelievably the hardest thing ever achieved by me
Yet it came so easily
Honestly,
It wasn't until this gift was seen by me
That I realized exactly what freedom really means to me
It was as if a key had been given to me
And I was able to unlock all the bars to the horrors that kept caged my misery!
I traveled to places and faced disgraces no other human being had seen;
My mind!
My heart!
My conscience!
I journeyed deep down into my soul
And it was an ugly scene to be!
I came to grips with the fact that such an iniquitous thing was me
I spent most of my lifetime chained to a hateful anger

But I was ignorant to it, so to me, it had just become a familiar stranger
Hate-filled, a hater, I even hated myself and didn't even know
Because I camouflaged that character defect with a supercilious ego
I acted like I more than loved me
I lived my life hella selfish, putting nothing above me
I was a slave to self-destruction and didn't even know
I thought I knew everything, but I didn't even know me though!
So, I lived my beautiful ugly life ignorant, unknowingly, regretting it so
Man, y'all just don't know what it was like to be me
To look dead into the mirror and love everything I see
While suffering so dreadfully underneath
All the while, in denial, of who I was supposed to be
Now I spend every damn day regretful and repenting
Repulsed by everything that I had been representing
There was a time in my mind when my shame was so painful
But then, I realized that my devil was meticulously murdering my angel
It was then that I woke up and started over again

I used this pen to poke a hole in my heart and pour out everything within
Up to that point I had been living my life pretending to be free
No longer a hostage to my hatred, the gift of writing released me
Now I close my eyes and cherish every image my minds-eye sees
I spill out my thoughts through writing, my deepest form of therapy
Heartfelt and sincere everything I write,
And I need that shit to be!
I unchain my pain and gift the world my brain
Now that's freedom to me!

Reflection

Freedom means different things to different people. This particular piece is me expressing how writing helped to liberate me from a self-destructive mindset that was hellbent on destroying me. When I say; freedom to me was unbelievably the hardest thing ever achieved by me, yet it came so easily, I am saying that freeing myself from the mental prison in which I had confined myself in for much of my life was one of the hardest things I ever did. But using writing as an outlet and a coping tool made it so easy in a lot of ways. I mean, to be able to go anywhere and do anything (as a writer) was so liberating! There were no boundaries when it came to the emotions and experiences I wanted or needed to explore. There were no limitations as to how deep I went when writing a poem or story. Writing taught me who I was born to be. Writing helped me work through and get past the most painful experiences of my life. Writing helped me learn about other cultures and to appreciate the differences in other people, it helped me to develop empathy and understanding, and it is one of the most liberating things I had ever experienced!

Hardest Poem I Ever Wrote

This poem here I start
With so much pain in my heart
Ashamed at the part
That I played in your life.
My role of being your father figure
Should've been so much bigger
You have no idea how many times I pulled out the "deadbeat" gun,
Put it to my head, and pulled the proverbial trigger
For the entire twenty-four years of your entire existence
I wasn't there for you, not nare instance
I couldn't provide for you any assistance
Son, please know that from the very first moment I went to jail
The only time a tear o' mine ever fell
Was when thoughts of you entered my mind in this unforgiving cell
And I had to sit there confined, mind dying, in my own personal hell

Young me, damn man!
I hope you understand man
Since you're now in the same predicament that I'm in
Son, if I could sacrifice these forty-seven years of my life
To remove every tear that ever fell from your eyes
I wouldn't hesitate for a minute
To walk up to that casket and hop up in it
Surely, as my salty tears stain this dampened page
I'm so overcome with my shameful rage
Angry at all the poor choices I ever made
Sorry for the price you and your daughter, my granddaughter, had to pay
But because I know you both love me so
I am able to cope
I am able to hope
Michael, this is the realest talk I ever spoke
I swear on my life, it's the hardest poem I ever wrote

Reflection

I wrote this poem to my son while he was prison. In my mind, it's because I wasn't the type of father I should've been that he went to jail.

It hurts to know that I directly impacted my only child's life in such a negative manner. When I was out there gangbanging, I put the thug life over my son's life, and I am deeply ashamed of being an absentee father.

I see my son going through the same things I went through, and still go through, when he talks to me about how much it hurts for him to be locked up and away from his daughter, my granddaughter. I feel his pain because I know it, because I understand it, because I lived with it. Most importantly, I feel his pain because I caused so much of it.

I say this is the hardest poem I ever wrote because of all the emotions I experienced when writing it. Coming face-to-face with my shame of not being a good father was a very painful endeavor.

I hope that when my son reads this it makes him see the importance of needing to be in his daughter's life, physically, emotionally, and in every other way possible.

I strive to be a positive example for him, so that he can be a positive example to my granddaughter. I am confident he will be a better father than I ever was.

The Tear That Wouldn't Drop

My father died last year
That's when I cried my last tear
Believe it or not
Only a single tear dropped
And it was a confused, conflicted, rebellious tear
Hard was it for that poor little tear to flow
For my angry eye to let it go
Because in my eyes
That sorry bastard had already died a long time ago!
Like I said,
A tear dropped my eye
A thing difficultly admitted
Ashamedly, I did it
Although he didn't deserve it
I felt I owed it to him
Because all my life
A son's love,
I never ever showed it to him
But how could I,

When he was never there?

How could I,

When it was him that I blamed for all of my despair?

How could I,

When I felt for so long that it was his fault my life was so fuckin' unfair!

Maybe now, since I better understand, and I've been there

Coupled with the fact that I never took it upon myself to clear the air

Or even barely care

Because I was so angry and hurt beyond my understanding

And I carried that hurtful pain with me everywhere!

I was able to see it from a different perspective

A mindset drastically altered after much deep reflection

And the more I thought of him, of them

The more that hurtful pain kept sinking in

I now know why I shed that confused, conflicted, rebellious tear

Because for the briefest of instances, I literally felt my father's pain

I intimately shared that man's shame

Because I was standing in shoes like his

And I was walking his pitiful path the same

Regardless of his failures

He was still my father
And in so many ways that kinda bothered
In essence
When he lost his life, a part of me died
And even though I never knew him
I feel I owed it to him
Because the father in me
Who for so long could never see
Understood exactly what it was like for him to be
And, that deep emotional outpour I couldn't stop
The tear that didn't want to drop

Reflection

This was a poem written after I lost my biological father, a man I never really knew. A man I discovered I cared for more than I wanted to admit. It still hurts for me to reflect on how I viewed my biological father throughout my lifetime. My father was a heroin addict who was absent from my life for nearly all of my life, at least ninety-nine percent of it. The couple of times he was in my life, it was never good. I remember one of the rare occasions when he was out of prison, my mother sent me to spend some time with him, a weekend or so. The only memory I have from that visit was him giving me a joint to hit and my getting high to a point it scared the hell out of me. He and his girlfriend were laughing at my expense while I was paralyzed with fear. I was eight years old! I don't have any memories of my biological father.

While I place a lot of the blame on him for my failures in life, I understand that I am ultimately responsible for my actions. Ultimately, I own all my shit! It doesn't clear him of his wrongdoing or relieve him of his guilt. As a kid I harbored some seriously ill feelings toward my biological father, and those feelings were manifested in my actions growing up. As a youth I veered so far off course that I became lost in the world. But as I grew up and matured in life, I realized I used a lot of my negative feelings as a crutch and an excuse to continue acting out negatively and being destructive. I was eventually faced with the challenge of growing up and getting real and right, or continuing to lose my fight with the demons within. Today I am victorious. I'm claiming that! I feel like I conquered my demons and am a much better person because of it. The tear that wouldn't drop finally fell, and when it did, it also released a lot of pent up negative feelings that allowed me to shed a lot of pain so that I could embrace the beauty of life and become my best self.

What Did You Expect of Me?

What did you expect of me?
When pushed out the womb so unexpectedly?
Can't blame mama at all
Because she never neglected me
While vicious ass whoopins on a regular basis
Only temporarily corrected me
Obviously, they failed to bring out the best of me
And with this seductive ass environment
Sittin' right here next to me
I embraced the thug life
And it eagerly accepted me
The street life was good
It was bomb just like sex to me
So, I did my thug thang, and I did it aggressively!
The lure of the impure was straight up like ecstasy
Intoxicated by it, I became delusional
And convinced myself that the rest of the world rejected me
With that thought in mind, slowly but surely, I morally

disconnected me
And I lived my life out of control
Packin' a pistol hella recklessly
An exact match out that six-pack when those frightened people selected me
Life in the penitentiary would be the next step for me
And without question, that would be the truest test of me
Because in my eyes, I'd finally become what everyone expected me to be
A fuckin' failure living up to my potential, just fulfilling my destiny
Fed up, I seriously considered suicide, almost quit and gave up
But my God protected me
He forced me to sit my ass down, and lean back in deep thought, reflectively
Then take a serious and honest inventory of the rest of me
"Be true to thine own self" became the deepest lesson to me
It also turned out to be the sweetest blessing to me
I did a lot of contemplative soul searching
And then concocted up a recipe
Meticulously, I fixed me up and reconnected me
I created a blueprint to a life lived successfully

Man, don't y'all know that I was blessed especially?

So now I ask you again, respectfully

What did you expect of me?

I hope nothing short of exceptionally

Because I'm definitely settin' up to be

Everything I was destined to be

This new improved version, that is the very best me!

Reflection

I don't have to explain what this poem means; it's self-explanatory. I tried to poetically summarize my journey thus far in life by posing the question "What Did You Expect of Me?" because most people didn't give me a chance when I was at my worst. Hell, some people didn't give me a chance when I first began displaying signs of being a troubled child exhibiting aggressive behavior. My journey was a rough one, filled with a lot of pain, disappointment and trauma. But at the end of the day, and after a lot of soul-searching and deep contemplation, I wrote this poem for two reasons, one; one; because no one expected much of me, so I wanted to highlight how negatively impactful that the, "he won't amount to anything." perspective is when presented to a young child already dealing with being traumatized and damaged; and two; until I determined that more needed to be expected of me, by me, then I would continue living up to everybody else's lowered expectations.

Creative Me

Don't Judge This Book By Its Cover

I am a book
Like no other
I stand here proudly
Prominent my display
I am full of intriguing, intelligent, and relevant things to say
At first glance you look upon me
And simply see my cover
Momentarily you're left to wonder
"Seems like so many others"
But then your curiosity is aroused
Inside, there's something fascinating you discover
You open me up carefully
Casually glossing over my table of contents
And then gradually, you get into me seriously
Understanding fully what I represent
You peruse my pages pleasurably
As I slowly reveal my life story
You bear witness to the core of me

Page after page, chapter after chapter
Joy tangled with pain; heartache intertwined with laughter
Touched by my story; you smile, you cry, at times
obscenities you utter
Your emotions give way to deep thought
That cause your heart to flutter
My pages are many
Seductive is my storyline
Complex yet exciting, unique and one-of-a-kind
Dark, thrilling, even mystifying at times
Creative and intricate is my beautiful concept design
My book comes in a hard-surfaced, rough-edged cover
But mine is a beautiful narrative nonetheless
Although extremely ugly at times, you helplessly lose
yourself in my mess
You're pleased by my honesty
Confused by my mystery
Amused with my humor
Taken aback by my history
All things considered, you enjoy me time and time again
Thankful that you took your time, studied me and
Discovered
I am a book
Like no other

Grateful,

That you didn't judge this book by its cover

Reflection

I vividly recall the day I wrote this poem! I had an appointment to be interviewed by an instructor who taught creative writing, and when I first entered her office to introduce myself, she looked at me like I was in the wrong place. She gave me this discriminatory look that made me feel like I was being racially profiled and stereotyped. When I told her that I was a writer who had written several books, her discriminatory look turned into one of incredulous disbelief. It wasn't the first time in my life that I felt discriminated against, but it was the first time as a writer I'd felt insulted and offended.

Initially I was angry and hurt, and I left that interview as pissed off as I'd been in quite some time. But the more I thought about it, the more those feelings of anger and hurt shifted to motivation and inspiration. I became more determined than ever to not only prove her wrong, but to also rub it in the faces of all the haters who ever told me that I couldn't, or wouldn't, amount to anything.

I wrote "Don't Judge This Book by Its Cover," and then soon after I wrote a novel called *Golden State Heavyweights*. When writing *Golden State Heavyweights*,

I specifically chose to create a character who had an astute and profound level of intelligence. In doing so I created Xavier Hightower, one of the coldest thugs you'll ever read about.

So, thank you to that particular creative writing instructor and to all the haters who didn't think that I'd ever amount to anything, for in this instance, no doubt, the haters were my motivators!!! As for the poem itself, I used the similarity and likeness of a book to illustrate and express the kind of person I see myself as being, the kind of person I am, and the kind of person you would come to know if you were to meet my acquaintance and get to know me free of any prejudices; without judging my book by its cover.

Roses That Grow from Concrete

Tupac Shakur aptly coined it
As The Rose That Grew From Concrete
Steadfastly I agree
Just like him, or you, or me
What I see,
Is a garden planted in these streets
True indeed,
There are the weeds
Sprouted up all over these bad seeds
Choking the life out of our communities
Plucked up and planted elsewhere
Go there with your despair
That self-hating, hurtful, hopeless air
But even you though I understand
So,
These words aren't meant to condemn
Instead, my focus is the roses
With a beautiful brilliance explosive
Eager to spread open their damaged petals

And be exposed to a positive prose
Undeterred by the pitfalls
They answered their calling when it called
Those roses,
Those beautiful Black roses,
Withstood the stormiest weather
They endured the scorching heat
And survived the trampling of ill-intended systemic feet
They grew strong and then they rose up
Their brilliance blossomed when opened up
So, beautiful Black roses
When you look back
See that garden, your community, with love and hope
And those roses,
The ones with a beautiful brilliance explosive
Reach back, show them some love, and then lift those ones up

Reflection

This poem was written as my way of paying homage to Tupac Amaru Shakur who, in my eyes, was one of the most artistic Black Men to walk this earth. His life was tragically cut short, and his full potential was never fully realized, but I sincerely believe that if he were still alive, he had the potential to become this generation's Malcolm X.

Tupac wasn't just a great rapper and actor, he was also a superb poet, and he inspired me. From day one he always spoke of the social ills and injustices that plague the Black community, and I respected and appreciated him deeply for that.

I referenced his poem "The Rose That Grew from Concrete" because it is a short but poignantly penned piece. And I wanted to pay tribute to him while talking about the many "Black Roses" growing in our concrete community. I wanted to especially focus on the Black Roses who aspire to do positive or great things with their lives in spite of the difficult circumstances and environments that systemic oppression has forced them to grow up in. I reference them when I speak about the people who were undeterred by the pitfalls, the ones who answered their calling when it called, because despite the many things that worked against them, they rose above their conditions and endeavored to be better.

In the end, I encourage those same Black Roses who make it out, to look back and see the garden that they came from (their community) with love and hope, and then reach back and lift other Black Roses up.

My Dear God

My dear God ...

You mercifully plucked me from the depths of my despair

You breathed a new life into me

And it was a righteous air

You provided me with a gift, a gift so rare

Your presence is inside of me

I feel you there!

My dear God ...

You opened my eyes

But even more so my heart

You deemed me worthy of a brand-new start

Yes, you took my misery

Wrapped it up, put it behind me and then made it my history

My dear God ...

You delivered me from the chaos

And gave me a choice

You gave me a voice!

This gift, this pen

To make a beautiful noise

To praise your name with poems so joyous

My dear God ...

I am thankful for your mercy

Grateful for this ink that serves the thirsty

No longer am I fearful of that which hurt me

And I give glory to you firstly

I beg of you oh Lord,

Forever, in your love immerse me

My dear God,

My dear God ...

Reflection

This poem is my praise to God, my thanking Him for blessing me with the gift of writing. This is also me giving thanks for His changing my heart, and changing my life because of it.

To All the King Pens and All the Queen Pens

In 1982 it all began
My fire got lit way back when
Mama came to visit me in juvenile hall, and she brought in
Two novels by two authors, two kings of the pen
The late great Donald Goines and Iceberg Slim
"Whoreson" and "Pimp; The Story of My Life"
Cut deep into my soul like a double-edged knife
At the young impressionable age of thirteen
African-American's, black men, brothas!
Writing about a lifestyle I'd personally witnessed and seen
It moved me in such a manner
Touched and affected me in such a way
I intellectually pillaged that small black village called
Holloway
Like so many of the characters those legends built up and
broke down with ink
And as sure as the eye blink
My ship became wrecked and slowly started to sink

My circumstance had me feelin' hopeless, I was on the brink
But like so many other brothas, I was raised up by some sistahs
And with my fire re-lit I recognized that this was it!
I discovered my gift and realized I too could do this!
It forever changed how I thought, the way that I would think
Sista Souljah, Teri Woods, Nikki Turner, Tracy Brown
Y'all were my connecting structure, my saving link
I have you, and so many other raw ass writers to thank
For motivating me to spin tales from the end of my pen
And poke holes in my emotion and pour out my wildest imagination
So, it's from the bottom of my heart that I tip my hat and say with that;
I extend my deepest appreciation
To all the King Pens, and to all the Queen Pens
For without you guys where would I be?
Perhaps just another fucked up character
Or quite possibly just another sad ass story

Refection

I wrote this poem as a tribute to writers everywhere, but especially to the writers who provided inspiration and motivation for me as I traversed the literary landscape trying to find my way as an author. But before I propped the writers, I made it a point to show some love to my mother because it was her who first truly introduced me to reading, which all these years later would in turn lead to me being the writer I am today.

When I was thirteen, I went to juvenile hall and my mother would visit me religiously, every single visiting day I could depend on my mother to be there, and I'll never forget how comforting it was for me because that was a very terrifying period in my life. It was my first time being in jail and I had never been away from my family, so no matter how tough I acted, I was really scared shitless. To help ease my mind my mother would bring books and magazines for me to read as a way of helping the time pass.

So, the first books I ever read for entertainment were Donald Goines and Iceberg Slim. Reading them lead to my reading other writers, but it was something about black men writing about some of the same type of stuff that was actually happening in the neighborhoods I grew up in that was more meaningful to my mental. It made me want to read everything Street-Lit, and at that time Holloway House was the only all-Black publishing house which sold those kinds of books. When I talk about pillaging that small black village called Holloway that's me paying respects to the publishing house that made today's Urban-Lit world possible.

When I break this poem down further people will gain a better understanding of exactly what some of the other stuff that I said means. For instance, I make the analogy of my ship becoming wrecked and slowly starting to sink much like the same way many of the characters in their books did. I was literally living the same kind of life that some of their characters were. Decades later, with the rebirth of Street-Lit, most of the books I was reading were written by sistahs, and much like the young black boys in the African-American community who grow up in single parent households, it's the Black woman who raises them, so I acknowledged the black woman and pay respects to the countless deserving sistahs who are forced to become father figures when too many of us brothas become absentee fathers. Sadly, I speak from personal experience

having gotten locked up and leaving my son's mother
alone to raise our son.
I end the poem by sending shout-outs to the many writers
who influenced or inspired me as I ventured into the
literary world alone. In a way, writing saved me from
having a bad ending to my own personal narrative, my life.
With writing being such a therapeutic tool, it has given me
an identity and a sense of self-worth like nothing else in
my life ever has. Writing has allowed me to dig deep and
discover who I am, as well as who I am not. It helped me to
define the type of "character" I would become in life. In
essence, reading and writing quite possibly saved me from
what could have been a bad ending to my life story.

June Bug & Roscoe; A Summer Day in the 70s

Wake up in the mornin' to the smell of bacon, eggs, and grits cookin'
Hurry up and do somethin' about the way he lookin'
Ain't heard nare word his loud mouthed lil sister sayin'
Grandma in her bedroom on bended knees prayin'
Marvin Gaye already the third album mama playin'
He woofed down breakfast and quickly asks for more
Quickly finishes that plate, quickly tending to his chores
Gotta hurry! Gotta hurry! Gotta hurry!
Outside there's a big ole world that needs to be explored
"June Bug! Hey June Bug! You up yet in there?"
Roscoe hollered out, seemingly appearing out of nowhere
Daddy under the car, in the front yard
Smokin' on a square, fixin' on a spare
"Boy, get yo' ass back inside and do somethin' wit' yo' hair!"
June Bug rushed back in and grabbed a pick
The red, black, and green one with the balled-up fist

Then he balled it up in his fist

Pick, pick, pat ... Pick, pick, pat ... Pick, pat, pat, pick ...

Hope daddy like this! June Bug thought as the screen door slammed shut

“Lil boy, don’t make me beat yo’ butt!”

“Sorry mama!”

“Make sure you get home before the streetlights come on!”

“Yes ma’am,” June Bug muttered, with a disgruntled groan

“Boy, don’t act grown! And take your sister wit' you!” she yelled, headed for the phone

June Bug and Roscoe were already gone

Every fifth house they passed had a homemade swing hangin’ from a tree

With a thick braided rope tied to a tire

And down near the corner, up a little bit higher

Click-clacks and old sneakers swung lazy from a telephone pole wire

June Bug and Roscoe; best friends since they were knee-high to a grasshopper

One dark as the midnight sky, the other one new penny copper

Best of friends these two, doin’ what best friends do

Bustin’ empty nickel bottles and shootin’ at old soda cans

With small rocks from slingshots made from hanger wire,

denim and rubber bands
A bunch of bug squishin', crawdad fishin', and off-key whistlin'
A whole lotta mischievous ambition and big dream wishin'
The hours passed fast as the time comes and goes
June Bug sadly looked toward the sky at the dusky orange setting sun's glow,
"I guess we better be headin' home Roscoe."
"Yeah, I know," Roscoe replied despondently, walkin' ever so slow, "Yeah, I know,"
Too swift another summer day in the 70s go
No white picket fences around there
But with white sticks they picked the fences without a care
Then they played "Bingo!" with every cool car that passed by
Tiring of that, they played "Bet you Can't Catch Me in a Lie!"
Finally, back on the block
Sticks turned to swords after slingshots get tucked into knee-high tube socks
Neighborhood kids screamin' loud playin' tag and hopscotch
"Roscoe you ever wanna leave here?" June Bug quizzed, wonderingly

"Nope."

"Are we still gonna be doctors when we grow up?"

"I hope."

"Do you think we'll ever be rich?"

"Nah, but I also don't think that we'll ever be broke."

"Race you to my front yard!" June Bug hollered

Four feet pitter-pattin' fast, slappin' hard the black tar

The both of 'em breathin' deep after simultaneously smackin' the car

"I won! I won!"

"No you didn't June Bug! Man, you cheated!"

"June Bug beat it! June Bug beat it!" lil sis joyously jumped up and down, repeating

"I told you."

The only judge June Bug needed

"Guess I'll be headin' home now, streetlights are comin' on."

"I'll see you tomorrow Roscoe," June Bug bid his friend adieu while scootin' lil sis along

Halfway across the street, Roscoe was already gone

Thinkin' 'bout how tomorrow was gon' hurry up and come on

Reflection

"June Bug & Roscoe; A Summer Day in the 70s" is simply a throwback poem illustrating how life was for many of us growing up in the 70s. While I had a lot of difficult times as a kid, I'd be lying if I said they were all that way. Like most people who come from abusive, dysfunctional upbringings, I have some good memories I am able to reflect on and smile about too. This is one of them.

This Particular Butterfly

This particular butterfly
Soft and lovely
Like a bedtime lullaby
I'd see her for weeks
Yet we'd never speak
But the first time we did
My heart skipped a beat
This particular butterfly
Walked with a confident swagger,
That was so fascinating
She talked with a sensuous charm,
That was so captivating
This particular butterfly
Was so intoxicating
She had flawless brown skin
With an hourglass frame
Every outfit she wore
Complimented that thang
Every step she took was like

Bang! Bang! Bang!
This particular butterfly was hot like flame
But what stood out most,
Was her intelligence!
But what stood out most,
Was her elegance!
But what stood out most,
Was her relevance!
This particular butterfly
Was so beautiful
And so remarkable
She was so heavenly
This exquisite Black butterfly is a Queen named Ebony

Reflection

"This Particular Butterfly" is a poem I wrote after meeting this beautiful sistah named Ebony. She had a way about herself that had me checkin' for her on a regular basis. She was hella pretty, but there were so many other qualities about her that were even more attractive than her looks. Her personality was the bomb! She was also very vulnerable and soft at times. She was extremely intelligent, and this woman was so damn sexy! Yeah, Ebony was so bad I had to write a poem about her!!!

I Am ...

I am
But one
Grain of sand
That populates this majestic land
Ingrained in this clay
This clay that is man
I am what I am ...

I am
But one
Drop of water
In this sea of life
Perhaps, a solitary teardrop of displeasure
From God's disappointed eye
But I am I ...

I am
But one
Shred of thread
In this existence that is our fabric
A complex underlying structure

Ready to rupture
If you can feel me, then you can touch us ...

I am
But one
Fleeting thought
Of a Supreme Being
Or maybe not
I am a little
I am a lot ...

I am
But one
Breath of air
I am here
I am there
I am everywhere
Yet, I am rare ...

I am
But one
Problem or solution
Failure or lesson
I am a blessing
I am but one

But one I am ...

Reflection

I wrote this poem as a way of expressing the importance of *me* to myself, and to also point out the importance of any single one of us on this earth. In the history of mankind, I see my existence as the equivalent to a grain of sand on the ground, or one drop of water in the sea, but as small, or unimportant, or insignificant as that may seem, my existence is momentous and meaningful! Just as your existence is momentous and meaningful!

I ended this poem with making a comparison to my possibly being a problem or a solution, a failure or a lesson, because at the end of the day the choices I make are mine. And when it's all said and done, I have more control than anyone else on how my life turns out based on those choices.

The Sky and I

It's a dark night
Black clouds dot a blue sky
The moon sly
Like a half-winked eye
My mood cries
As I wonder why
Alone I sit
The sky and I
My pained spirit screams out silently
My heart beats about so violently
My tear drops fall down defiantly
Why did my truth have to always lie to me!?
I'm only left to wonder why
Alone I sit
The sky and I
While the stars huddle here and there
A captive audience to my despair
Quiet clouds gather
Slow to roam

A silent witness

To my bemoan

But comforting is its companionship

Enriched by it

They eventually enliven my spirits

And many of my sorrows soon do die

Alone I sit

The sky and I

Reflection

I literally wrote this poem in my head as I looked up into the sky and processed some of the shit I'd been going through during a difficult time in my life. When I gazed up into the late evening sky, this is what I saw as I processed my emotions and dealt with the pain of feeling helpless and hopeless. Sitting in prison with a life sentence makes a man wonder often if he'll ever regain his freedom, or if it is his fate to die in there.

Sometimes when you're going through something, the best company you can have is your own thoughts and the natural setting around you. Find peace from within and in your surroundings. For me, at the time, it was "The Sky and I."

It's Summer Time and It's Freezin'

Fearlessly, I walk countless laps around this depressing ass prison yard
Mad as fuck at the entire world
My cold corrupted heart callous and scarred
I'm forever lookin' hard
My mean mug looks painted on like an angry ass tattoo
And it's always aimed directly at you
On the other side of the fence and shiny wire that's barbed
With a gun in hand, stands a hate-filled guard
And he posted up like a statue
At the slightest transgression ready to gat you;
Splat you!
Bless you with a bullet to the brain, if you so much as sneeze;
Ha-chew!
I'm surrounded by evil-intentioned gangstas with hard frames like body builders
Dope dealers, dope fiends, bold stealers and cold killers
Deep seated the hate, the deeply rooted animosity that

saturates
Whilst a dense anger hovers somewhere in the air
Fear, hate, and regret, always lingering near
Mixing with the potent weed smoke floating up there, just barely evident
The greedy insatiable need to be freed is ever so relevant
Whether it be the beast within
Or the beast that is within each and every one of them
A byproduct of the gang and racial tension that's always here
Thick, like piles of shit, in this toilet bowl atmosphere
A six-inch screw with a ripped bedsheet for a handle in my waistband,
And I'm packin' it like a gun
One hand always near it as I coolly soak up the sun
As my suspicious eyes dispassionately take in all the fun
One must always be aware of the pokerfaced greetings
Followed by hush-hush, out in the open, in-the-cut meetings
Some form of disrespect usually the reason
Prison politics is twisted and sick,
But a requirement many must fear
When those greetings, followed by meetings
Are the result of an unlucky fool's treason

Its summer time and it's freezin'
The sizzling mid-afternoon sun was unrelentingly beamin'
But the penitentiary is a cold, frigid world, and it's killing season!
Mind your own, keep it movin' and keep it breathin'
"Yard down! Everybody down! Inmate, drop that weapon!"
A loud, imposing command heard far too often
I calmly lie down and stretch out in some unfortunate convict's coffin
A damn shame; some poor fool just got caught with his guard down
In a pool of blood, he laid splayed out on the unsympathetic ground
Maybe he got caught slippin' while lost in his thoughts
He might be alive.
But by the way he ain't moving, he might not
Some guilty cat cheesin' while coolly wiping a splash of blood off the tip of his boot
As the unlucky fallen fool keeps wheezin' difficultly
Between exhausted moans and irrepressible soft poots
Life
Slowly slipping
Away

Ice Mike

Stripped down to our boxers,
The guards search every inmate while the rest of us relax and sunbath
Casual conversation of the norm ensues for hours,
On a sinister graveyard that's half-dirt, half-paved
Just another day in the fray while the incorrigible misfits misbehave
It's a sad reality, but this type of tension ain't ever leavin'
At least, not in these cruelly constructed California prisons
That too many Black and Brown folks be tightly squeezed in
No matter the time of year,
And regardless of the season
This broken justice system cooks them and then feed them
To the Belly of the Beast,
Where, it's always summer time and it's always freezin'

Reflection

This poem, while artfully illustrated, is an extremely ruthless reality that *every* inmate in *every* prison on the planet is confronted with. And while I haven't been to any prisons outside California, I have done enough time in several California prisons to know that the California Department of Corrections promotes and fosters these exact types of violent environments with a purpose: taking advantage of a lot of men and women who have already been severely traumatized. Many people, inmates in particular, believe that this is an intentional practice by the California Department of Corrections for the purpose of maintaining job security and a lifestyle they have become all too comfortable with. It is also a part of the deviously designed Prison Industrial Complex's way to keep alive a form of systemic oppression that reaps huge benefits for today's *plantation owners* (investors and stock holders in the largest prison system on the planet).

Color Coded

My Rainbow

I am made up of many colors
None of which are just one of me
For I am comprised of an array of hues
And these are the sum of me
These colors are representative
Of the characteristics that define me
Behind, all of these colors combined
Somewhere you will surely find me
You see, the blue is my cool
The serene, calm, and collected I
That bright red is the angry, upset or frustrated I
And that deeper shade of red
Is the passionate, fiery, hot-blooded guy
The yellow there you see
Just barely, and ever so rarely
It's actually present more than I'd like to admit it
It's the fearful and scared me
The gray area that is there
I'm still trying to define it
I think it's me divided
Maybe my two sides undecided
This green is my ambition

My competitive drive and constant desire
To achieve success at a thing
And continuously strive to reach higher
But ahh, behold!
My precious gold
That's my swagger, my confidence, my bold
It's the beautiful aura that always surrounds me
I'm immersed in its richness
To the point sometimes it almost drowns me
The white tinge you see
That is the fair me
Slightly discolored I dare agree
But it allows me to see
This dark world with much more clarity
The brown represents the stained me
Evidence of the pained me
My ugly
My afflicted
My ashamed me
And finally, but most definitely
Yes ultimately!
The Black you see
It's the color God chose when He sculpted me
It's the color of my strength

My toughness

My resilience

It's the color that shines with the brightest brilliance

My Black is my honorable

My proud

My dutiful

My Black is my beautiful

These many different shades

These colors that shine bright and always glow

They are me

Who I'll always be,

They are my rainbow

Reflection

"My Rainbow" is a reflection of what a rainbow is: a colorful energy that represents a beautiful ending to an ugly beginning. I used colors to give a descriptive account of the many shades of who I am, the many different layers of me.

Here's a breakdown of each color:

Blue is a color one associates with being mellow or having a calming effect, like blue skies or blue waters, so blue is my cool.

Red is often described when one is angry; "He's seeing red." I used this illustration to identify the side of me that too often was too quick to surface. Red is also a hot color, so I describe the passionate side of myself with a brighter shade of red.

Yellow is a color people once used when describing a coward. I personally think that, at one time or another in our lives, we've all had a coward inside of us. When I reference this color it simply explains the scared or fearful side of me. I say "barely" and "ever so rarely" because, as a man, it was difficult to admit that I was afraid of something. It's how many of us (boys/men) are raised to think. But in truth, we're all afraid at one time or another.

I'm just no longer afraid to admit that.

The color gray is tricky, but very significant. We often talk about "gray areas", meaning unclear or uncertain situations. Being half Black and half White, I grew up feeling very awkward because I struggled with being mixed in a predominantly Black environment. I had a lot of identity issues that were the root cause of some of my childhood troubles. So, I use gray to speak of the two sides of me most affected by being mixed, which is in essence all of me: my Black side -my white side, my good-my bad, my beautiful-my ugly.

Green is the color of money, the one thing people most associate with success.

Gold is the color of bling, so I use it to describe my swag, the part of me that people saw first and foremost for much of my life, not knowing that it was a fictitious act on so many occasions. It was my defense mechanism.

When I refer to the color white, I'm talking about the half-white side of me. Being mixed I felt somewhat tainted growing up because I had no awareness of self, or that side of my family. In my journey to find out who I truly am, I discovered I had nothing to be ashamed of. In fact, it was during this soul-searching mission that I found out who I really was, and fortunately for me I was able to redefine

myself.
Brown is a color I used to describe what I once considered "the stained me". My ugly, my afflictions, my personal shames are the worst kinds of stains in my life. And finally, Black, or my Blackness; although I am mixed, I've always considered myself to be Black, as does the world. But being Black is so much more than a color God chose me to be. Being Black is a state of mind. It's a unique attitude and disposition. It's an unexplainable essence that shows up and shines brightest when faced with the most troubling adversity. There are no people in the world like Black people, it's why every other race on the planet tries to emulate us and replicate the positive creativeness of Black culture. But none of those other races dare desire to experience the Black struggle because they're not built like us, they are not designed to deal with and overcome the kinds of trauma and evil that Black people have been dealing with and overcoming for hundreds of years. That's why I say that my Black is the color that shines with the brightest brilliance, because through all of the pain and suffering that I've been forced to endure, I overcame it, and I am still shining!

Beautiful Black Bird

Fancy yourself a beautiful Black bird
High up in the tree of life you sit, perched
Afraid and unknowing
While your intelligent mind and good heart search
Find yourself, look deeper within
Try, and if at first you fail, then try again
Discover who you are, and where it is you want to go
Search your heart especially
Because surely the heart knows
See that dream clear, without fear, beyond brave eyes closed
Don't be afraid to spread your wings wide
And fly
Flap hard and fly high
Rise,
And rise,
And rise!
A beautiful Black bird in flight
Oh, what a wonderfully magnificent sight

When you catch that jet-stream called life and soar
Never to be afraid to fly high anymore
Your boundaries are limitless
You can own the skies
Because you are a beautiful Black bird, is why
So, fly,
And fly,
And fly high!

Reflection

This poem is a dedication to Black people everywhere, especially my amazingly wonderful granddaughter, Saniyah.

This poem is a positive reinforcement and an expressed encouragement to Black people everywhere!!!

A Black Fire Still Burning

Long before cruelly constructed manacles bound the limbs of royalty
Sick, immoral minds
Sat huddled in cozy confines
Conspiring an evil disloyalty
A beautiful people
Violently ushered into a never-ending anguish
Inhumanely sailed and ruthlessly propelled
Into a permanent purgatory to forever languish
The whole of a soul to be sold like stock
Made to parade these slaves minus dignity
On pitiless podiums called auction blocks.
The stinging crack of a wicked white master's whip
Another crack comes again and again quick
African blood spilled
Fast to pour
A slow dribble downward onto the stolen, star-spangled floor
Black skin rips while red blood drips countless times more

Dark faces stand 'round forced to bear witness

Whilst smiling pale visages gather, but only to cheer this

Lessons demonstrated by a heartless devil;

Men emasculated

Women raped

A beautiful people filled with an ugly hate

A destructive loathing we can't escape

Mindsets changed, forever shaped

A contemptable condition has become our fate

A horror no words can ever distinguish

A Black fire still burning

No amount of time will ever extinguish

Reflection

I wrote this because white America continues to need a reminder of what it is that they have done to an entire race of people, and how what they did and continue to do, is still destructive to that same entire race of people.

While it's very easy and convenient to play the "I wasn't there when it happened" card, white people who play that card don't seem to mind reaping the benefits of the privilege that came off the backs of Black people who were there.

Crimes against humanity don't have a statute of limitation, yet no one seems to be remotely interested in prosecuting America for its unrivaled criminal history.

It's Outrageous!

It's outrageous
The way they played us
Throughout the ages
It took place in stages
Check your history book pages!
They came to invade us
Then they made us get in cages
Shackled us and chained us
All this to enslave us
From the blackest to the beigest
They would parade us
And then proudly display us
Only to sale and trade us
Mercilessly beat us and rape us
On our lacerated backs their vile draped us
Now they act like centuries of complex trauma ain't suppose to faze us
40 acres and a mule
The price and promise they proposed to pay us

But systemic oppression, pure hell and a jail cell

Was all they actually ever gave us

And they have the nerve to hate us

It's crazy!

They even found a new way to plague us

Poverty, subpar education, and AIDS

That's how they aided us

Crack cocaine, another evil instrument used to bait us

Now they raid us with gauges

And tase us or just blaze us

Unfair sentencing laws devastate us

Incriminate and discriminate us

Their plan-B;

Put us in the system and let the system raise us

They even figured out a way to teach us to hate us

Now self-hate has become ridiculously contagious

And no longer outraged are us

This is outrageous!

It's outrageous ...

Reflection

This is a poem I wrote as a way of venting and releasing some of the radical thoughts and feelings that I had as a young person, and some that I still have today. Growing up as a mixed child in a predominately Black neighborhood was very hard for me. At the time, I didn't know how devastating my identity issues were, but as I got older and gained a better understanding, I was able to comprehend why I had developed so many negative characteristics and viewpoints. Repeatedly being shown and told through media and racist action that Black is not beautiful, and hearing Black people always talk negatively about "the white man" who was oppressing them made me fucked up in the head. These are some of the sentiments I felt a strong need to express at a time in my life when I needed to get some shit off my chest that had been present for as long as I can remember.

Black people have lived in and grown up in a nation that has *always* tried to keep us on the bottom of the totem pole, and to this day white America continues to use every diabolical tactic possible to disparage and destroy the African-American people.

If you feel like something I said in this poem, or reflection, is inaccurate or false, I say to you; "It's Outrageous!" It's outrageous that you can be so blind and ignorant to the truth!

Colors

Bloods wrapped in red
Shoot at Crips dipped in blue
Retaliation is a must
So, sadly, the reverse order holds true
And regrettably, this destructive cycle continues to continue
Now families dressed in black
Watch their loved-ones lowered in brown holes six-feet deep
The yellow, pink, and white floral arrangements
Do nothing to ease the pain
Of the bowed heads and tear-stained faces of those loved ones that weep

Reflection

"Colors" is the result of a writing exercise I was challenged to do when I was incarcerated. I like to think outside of the box when doing writing prompts, so instead of writing a piece on colors that would be of the cookie cutter variety, I chose to write this piece based on the Blood and Crip culture I grew up in and was heavily involved with for a number of years. It's a very ugly narrative that needs to be highlighted so that we as a people (African-Americans) can at some point turn the mirror on ourselves so we can stop destroying ourselves.

Black Girl

Black girl
Be proud
Walk tall
Speak loud
Stand out in the crowd
Be true to you
And all you do
Create your own style
When the hater's hate
And the clown's clown
Keep doing you,
Show that beautiful smile
Ignore their ugly growl
Pay no mind to their foul
That ignorant, insecure vile
Don't you know you were born a blessed child?
You are a Queen!
Proudly wear your crown
And right here, right now

To your own self vow
To hold your own self down
And to be your best version
In every way, and every how!
Because,
You're a beautiful Black girl
And you should ALWAYS be proud!

Reflection

"Black Girl" is another poem written with the intention of uplifting Black girls and Black women everywhere. Having come to a greater understanding of what it is that my sistahs have been through, and continue to go through, motivated me to write something that championed their circumstance and offered supportive words to let them know there are countless Black men who respect and honor them, appreciate and support them, and are willing to protect them.

Black girls and Black women go through so much shit on a daily basis! And I felt like it's only right to let them know that I love my beautiful Black Sistahs ...

Lions Not Lambs!

I stand with my hands
Fist balled, like damn!
I do not understand
And I cannot comprehend
How you mark me with this brand
That is all a part of your scam
To brainwash me and
Convince me that I am
Less than a man
Even lesser than human
Because my skin tone is tanned
But I've learned who I am
I've allowed my mind to expand
And as a result of being woke
I will be damned
If I go along with your plan
Because I refuse to pretend
That your actions don't offend
I will gladly stand

On any stage that is grand
And proudly, hella loudly
Declare to every man
And every woman in this land
Who is darker than
Any one of them
That we are lions not lambs!

Reflection

"Lions Not Lambs" is a poem that illustrates my thoughts and feelings as they relate to the racist white supremacist systems that have been in place since the birth of America. I once had a *lamb* mindset, meaning that I saw myself as being less than and not worthy as a young Black boy/man. I may not have verbalized those sentiments, but my actions demonstrated this mentality completely. Now, since becoming woke, I have developed a *lion* mindset, meaning that I know who I am, and I fully understand that I am a powerful force on this earth as a Black man! I know my worth, and I am hella proud to be Black, I am very understanding of the systems that are still in place, systems which continue to undermine the African-American community. And because of this understanding, I tirelessly work with our young people so that they too can be "Lions Not Lambs."

Damaged Goods

I look deep into your eyes
And my heart cries for you
Because,
For the life of me
I can't understand
Why you don't see what it is that I do
I guess,
The beautiful package you came so splendidly wrapped in
Is to you,
A tortured temple that you feel severely trapped in
Surrounded by walls of judgement screaming, "too thick" or "too thin,"
Encased in barriers "too this" or "too that" concerning your beautiful Black skin
You think pitiful your beautiful, as though you are damaged goods
But to me, Queen, what I see
Is the epitome of what beauty is supposed to be!

Reflection

This poem is meant to uplift Black Queens everywhere, particularly the sistahs who struggle with self-confidence and feel like they have to change their truth to appease the world's lie. For centuries, Black women have been made to feel as if their natural beauty doesn't quite measure up. Well, this is my way of saying to all my Black Queen's that you are beautiful as you are. You have to believe it! Because my words don't have a single cent of value if you don't see yourself as beautiful.

Black-On-Black Crime

When you hear the words "Black-on-Black crime,"
A thugged-out African-American may come to mind
Poppin' slugs at his own kind
Swappin' drugs with his own kind
Robbin' and muggin' his own kind
But Black-on-Black crime is so much deeper than that
Allow your mind to grasp a concept much steeper than that
Its birthplace was in the confines of a slave-owner's plantation
Who could've ever predicted the eventual ramifications?
You see, when the white slave-owner planted his seed
He did it in more than one way indeed
He planted a self-destructive morsel of hatred and greed
And then those corrupted seeds sprouted up into trees
Trees that produced many branches which grew many leaves
And plenty of rotten fruit they did conceive
But oh what a tangled web he'd weave
Because, the fruit don't ever fall far from the tree

Reflection

"Black-On-Black Crime" is a poem written as a rebuttal to the racist and discriminatory term coined by white America through mass media in the '80s and '90s. There are no similar terms used when describing crimes that involve individuals of other ethnicities who commit crimes against their race. This is simply another way that white America tries to subliminally (or not so subliminally) brainwash people, especially African Americans. I wanted to highlight how crime and hatred were introduced and taught to the Black man in America by slave owners and white citizens who raped, robbed, defiled, and destroyed the Black population since its inception. Crime is a learned behavior. Hate is an emotion that was presented to the Black man on a daily basis on the most extreme levels possible, for centuries! So, as far as I'm concerned, when Black people began committing crimes in America, they were simply acting out learned behaviors. And since we were also taught by white America to hate ourselves, it's no wonder why Black people harm other Black people. Then when you throw in all the ways that systemic oppression negatively impacts Black people, you begin to understand how the seeds that were planted in the confines of slave owners' plantations conceived a rotted fruit that never fell far from its tree. The fruit is now rolling all over America's blood-stained ground ...

Kool Wit' That

My goonish buffoonery
Makes a cartoon of me
And I'm kool wit' that

Rude ignorant bastard
My anger gets lost faster
And I'm kool wit' that

Uneducated and illiterate
Don't even consider it
And I'm kool wit' that

Untrustworthy scandalous thief
Will lie through my teeth
And I'm kool wit' that

Pockets empty I stay broke
Comfortable living off other folk
And I'm kool wit' that

Got kids I don't even know
Couldn't care less how they grow
And I'm kool wit' that

Plenty of sex wit' no protection
Play Russian roulette with my erection
And I'm kool wit' that

My mentality is I don't care
My faults and fallacies I'm well aware
And I'm kool wit' that

Disrespect my sistahs and hate my brothas
Don't dare care about nare other
And I'm kool wit' that

It's a proven fact
As a people, Black folks, we are doing that
Our love for self, we are losing that
Man, the truth hurts
Damn, we need work
So that foolish act?
Let's be through wit' that
And then be Kool Wit' That
BE KOOL WIT' THAT!!!

Reflection

I wrote this poem to shine a light on a mentality that is all too prevalent throughout the African-American community.

Personally, I feel like we've gotten to a point where ignorance and all of its trappings have become an acceptable way of life in too many parts of the world we live in. Disrespectful conduct and self-deprecating behavior is being glamorized, while proper conduct and respectful mannerisms are frowned upon.

I feel like I can speak on this particular issue from the standpoint I do because I once use to think and act in a very ignorant and self-deprecating way. I literally used to think that it was kool to be a fool, and growing up in an environment where that way of thinking is all too common, I realize how "lost in the sauce" some of our brothas and sistahs are. And they think that there's nothing wrong with it!

Over the years I've learned that it's easier to make a point, or get a point across, if you bring an issue to a person using an "I" statement as opposed to a "YOU" statement. So rather than come across as being preachy or giving the impression that I am attacking someone, I approach this poem from a 1st person POV (point of view) and I use self as an example while pointing out some of the more negative issues that are affecting society, more specifically the African-American community.

This is just my way of saying, in an artful form, we need to change our way of thinking; because when you change how you think, you change the way you act; when you change the way you act, you change the way you live, and when you change the way you live you change the world.

It's All Love

My Deepest Devotion

You light up my darkest days
With your bright smile and your beautiful ways
I appreciate the fact
That you appreciate me
And that,
Makes me want to give you my all
Cherish your perfections
And embrace your every flaw
I want to give you my best
Write your name across my chest
For life too
Wife you
I met you and I've been better ever since
Because we make so much sense
And it's so damn intense!
From the start we flowed
My part became whole
My heart and my soul
Completely, you complete me
Baby, you are my glow
Beautiful, sexy, intelligent and wise
Your body is like art to my eyes

And yet, you're magnificent like a sunset

I love you because you inspire my deepest emotions

You loved me for me

And for that,

You've acquired my deepest devotion

Reflection

Like most of my love-related poems, I wrote "My Deepest Devotion" to express a side of myself which had gone without true love all of my life. The hopeless romantic in me refused to be suppressed anymore, so I devised ways like this in which to express how I saw love "in a perfect world." My hope is to one day find a woman who inspires my profoundest emotions and earns my deepest devotion.

What Is Love?

Love is ...
The feeling that overwhelms me every time I am next to
you
The fact that I know the worst of you
Yet, all I will ever see is the very best in you

Love is ...
The rush of excited emotions that only you are able to
provide me
Small explosions of my truest emotions
That erupt repeatedly in places deep inside of me

Love is ...
The smile in your eyes, the music in your laughter
The softness of your loving touch
Your tender kisses that keep me caught up in your rapture

Love is ...
All of the instances when I look at you
How I love it, 'cause you're not even conscious of it
When I discover something new in you

Love is ...
Getting to know every bit of you, and still wanting more
Intimately touching you at your deepest core
Love is making you purr with pleasure after making you roar

Love is ...
Doing it the way we do
Tasting every inch of you, savoring everything about you
It's becoming one with you, and then feeling like I'm none without you

Love is ...
Surrendering my heart to you, and hating ever having to be apart from you
Pissin' you off, feudin' wit' you, arguing too
And then realizing even the thought of that is hard to do

Love is ...

Facing life's difficult challenges and standing side by side when we do it

Remembering our promises of the heart

And regardless of how hard it gets, forever staying true to it

Love is ...

The moments where I won't be able to stand you

Yet I will always understand you

It's this trust, this respect, this friendship I have with you

It's patience, its loyalty, its honesty

It's hard, it's easy, it's crazy, it saved me!

It's the bad, the ugly, and the good too

What is love?

Love is me and you ...

Reflection

Love is a question to be answered by the individual experiencing it. I compare the feelings of love to a lot of things, in a lot of ways. What is love to you? That's a question that only you can answer.

Beautiful

When I met you
The word beautiful was vividly defined
It became clear to me
The moment we first conversed
Unrehearsed
The smile that melted my heart
Along with the bright twinkle in your eye
That captured my fascination
And made me want to know; who, what, when, and why
It was as if our souls had touched
A soft, sweeping, yet gentle brush
But it was enough!
Your magnetic pull moved me so much
And it kept my curiosity aroused like a teasing touch
The more of you that was revealed to me
The more beautiful you became
Your one-of-a-kind personality evoked emotions in me I can't explain
Your aura was so warm

It was as if it glowed
Your beauty was unmatchable
Amazing and fantastical
Remarkable like it was magical
A beauty exquisite and wonderfully natural
You possess a special quality
That brings out the best of me
Before I met you all of this was simply unimaginable
To even consider flirting with the notion
That this giddy feeling still existed
But there's no doubt about it, you have it
That "it" factor
Your charm, your joyous laughter, your profound passion
Your wisdom, your patience, your enduring understanding
I could go on forever describing the virtuous attributes I see in you
But in one word, put simply, you are
Beautiful

Reflection

"Beautiful" is my way of expressing my romantic side in the guise of prose.

It's a description of how I imagine feeling, or have felt, when a woman captures my attention in a way that isn't surface. And since beauty is in the eye of the beholder, this is my perspective on the many different aspects that make a woman beautiful.

I intentionally chose not to focus on any of the typical "physical" attributes when writing this poem, because to me the ultimate definition of a woman being beautiful is much deeper than what they possess physically.

For me, a woman has to possess the ability to move me on numerous levels.

Beautiful is being able to converse with a woman on a deeper level than normal, a level that stimulates me mentally and intellectually.

And then to be able to appreciate and enjoy so many other things about her at the same time: her attitude, her confidence, her energy, her aura, her fashion sense, her mindset, and her overall disposition among other things.

Yeah, that's what beautiful is to me.

I Hate You Love!

I hate you love!

Because you make me so possessive

And that truly irks me

I mean, you make me so obsessive

And you always seem to hurt me

I hate you love!

Because you don't play fair

And you don't ever seem to care

Nowhere near as much as I dare

Not to mention you seem so damn rare

I hate you love!

Because when I want you

You are never there

When I didn't want you

You are everywhere

And when I finally have you

It's like you're not even here

I hate you love!

Because you make me do the dumbest things

And I know that I am smart
Plus, you always break my heart
And you don't just break it
You tear my heart apart
I hate you love!
Because I can't figure you out
As soon as I think I do
I realize I don't have a clue
You confuse me to the point
I just don't know what to do
Yeah, I hate you love
But damn it I love to hate you!

Reflection

This is me being angry at love, yet still loving love, even though sometimes I hate it.

Poetry Is ...

Poetry is ...
Our very first conversation
Our very first private revelation
Our very first hug
Our very first kiss
Poetry is ...
Me being everything that you need and want
You being everything that I ever missed
Our unconditional acceptance of one another
The sweetest bliss!
Poetry is ...
The smile in my heart that's been present since I met you
You being a part of my every thought, making it impossible to forget you
Those oh-so-intimate sentiments of me that find space and time in your mind
Especially the ones that leave you breathless, and yes, sometimes even wet too
Poetry is ...

Understanding that you have demons, same as I do
Being open-minded to the fact, that, both of our skeletons have their own issues
Yet, here we sit with this once-in-a-lifetime opportunity to be anything that we wish to
Poetry is ...
These unbreakable bonds that are now being formed
These promises of the heart that are now being sworn
Building a strong and solid foundation
Designed to weather and withstand the mightiest of storms
Poetry is ...
Taking your heart to places it has never been
And then, making your heart explode with happiness over and over again.
Poetry is breathtaking
Poetry is so right
Poetry is us alone under the stars and moonlight
Poetry is absolute love
Poetry is unbridled lust
Poetry is incredibly romantic
Poetry is us ...

Reflection

I wrote "Poetry is ..." to explain how I feel when I am in love or falling in love. It is the truest expression of my heart and the best description of what falling in, or being in love is like for me. I am poetry; you are poetry; we are poetry; everything that we experience in our lives is poetry! But there is no more beautiful form of poetry than when two hearts become one, and love is the reason.

Michael's Haikus

While recently facilitating a creative writing workshop at a youth center, I became aware of and interested in a Japanese form of poetry known as haiku. After learning what a haiku is and then seeing how thought provoking, creatively challenging, and cool it was to me, I became more intrigued in this Japanese form of poetry. I wanted to see how deep and meaningful I could be while only using seventeen syllables, especially knowing that I could only use five syllables on the first line, seven on the second, and five again on the third line. The following are a dozen haikus I chose to write specifically for this book.

In this particular section I use different themes to write my haikus about ...

(My Life in a Haiku)

Nineteen sixty-nine

A beautiful tragedy

This cold life of mine

(My Being an Author)

Behind my eyes closed

Amazing daydreams captured

Now books in time froze

(A Tribute to Tupac's "The Rose That Grew from Concrete")

A beautiful rose

From cold concrete, I suppose

In full bloom I chose

(Complimenting a Beautiful Woman)

Her smile like sunshine

Brilliant and lovely her mind

She's one of a kind

(My Future Wife)

Waited all my life
She's bad, smart, and beautiful
She's my future wife

(My Mother)

The reason I'm here
Her love unconditional
My mother, my dear

(Giving Back)

I took so much peace
My debt paid, now redeemed, so
I give my best me

(Theory on Life)

I came and I went
I came, I saw, I conquered
My past and present

(Homage to My Ancestors)

The horrors endured

Sacrificing you for me

I'll always owe thee

(My Life)

To breathe in sunshine

And smile wide with joy each time

My life is just fine

(My Son)

From his first breath breathed

A splendid thing, this young King

My beautiful seed

(A Revolution!)

Time for change has come

By way of voice, or the gun

A revolution!

Mental Musings

No human being was designed to be confined in isolation for prolonged periods of time, no, not even the savage man, with a savage mind.

- *Ice Mike*

Solitary Mentality

I was forced to function under a solitary mentality at a very young age. I didn't have a choice; I had to. My survival depended on it. Forming a solitary mentality was critical in my efforts to cope with the traumatizing conditions that were forced upon me. My first taste of "solitary confinement" came as a five-year-old when my stepfather forcefully stuffed me behind the refrigerator because I wouldn't stop crying after one of his many violent beatings. Being tightly wedged between the kitchen wall and that massive immovable object for hours on end was my first experience of imprisonment. For a five-year-old child who had already suffered years of abuse and was complexly traumatized to the core, this added element of torture was, literally, the epitome of "cruel and unusual punishment." It was at this time that I first formed my solitary mentality.

While in prison twenty years later, and after countless trips to solitary confinement, my solitary mentality was entrenched with an odd mixture of creative concepts, destructive thoughts, bad intentions, and extremely imaginative coping behaviors. When locked inside that cell, alone with my thoughts and with my anger fueling the violent vehicle that drove me to my destructive destinations, it was just a matter of time before someone or something pushed my button and turned my violent volume all the way up.

Venture back with me to a dark period in my life ...

Clank!

The cell door slammed shut and I stood inside the dank, empty room with my bedroll tucked tightly under my left arm and an angry scowl painted on my face. The handcuffs pinching the skin on my wrist only further aroused my anger as I seethed over the circumstances that had led to solitary confinement: a fight with another inmate in the chow hall over how he put potatoes on my tray. My chest inflated and deflated with every breath I took as I mean-mugged the paint-chipped, graffiti-tarnished walls with deep acrimony in my severely incensed eyes.

"Back up to the tray slot and put your hands out, palms up," the guard who'd escorted me to the hole commanded in an authoritative tone. I inwardly scoffed at the tough tone in his voice and took half a step backward, bending slightly at the waist. My closed fists easily found the tray slot and I pushed my hands out and opened my fists, my palms up. One by one each cuff was unlocked and removed, and the circulation in my arms returned to its normal flow.

Clank!

The tray slot slammed shut, and the jingling sound of the guard's keys faded as I slowly rubbed the reddish indentations on my wrists with the bedroll still tucked under my arm.

I pulled my shirt off and placed it on the end of the mattress, then sat my bedroll on top of it. "Nasty ass ma'fuckin' cell," I muttered under my breath as I ripped my raggedy state towel in half and got to work washing the entire cell down, using water from the stainless-steel sink and the bar of state soap they'd given me with my lockup kit. After cleaning the cell, I took a bird bath and then made my bed. As soon as my head hit the mattress somebody had the fuckin' nerve to attempt to talk to me.

"Aye cell 105, where you from homie?" a deep voice asked from what I guessed to be about four doors down the tier. He had broken off the conversation he was having with another inmate to inquire about my gang credentials.

It was standard hole protocol to hit the new guy up, so

I wasn't offended by his question. However, while I had been cleaning the cell, I'd overheard snippets of his conversation with another inmate, and based off the shit he'd said I'd already formed an opinion: I didn't like him, flat out. Having done so much "hole time" over the past twenty years, I could peep when somebody was fronting and putting on a hard facade by talking a bunch of rah-rah shit in an attempt to impress or intimidate the new guy on the block. On this occasion, the new guy happened to be me. The clown four doors down was one of those frontin' types.

I ignored the question, closed my eyes and focused on going to sleep. When he posed the question to me again, I ignored him again. I was intent on catching some Z's and sleeping my anger off. I needed to get lost in my imagination.

"That fool must be hella scared or somethin' homie. He ain't even representin' where he from!" the clown four doors down mockingly exclaimed to his homeboy when he didn't get the response he desired.

Sleep kidnapped my consciousness as my anger bubbled and my mind plotted doing bad things to the tough-talking cell soldier four doors down.

For the next nine days the cell soldier either directly

quizzed me about who I was and where I was from, or he circuitously directed offensive innuendos aimed at me when conversing with his homeboy.

I remained silent the entire time: plotting, scheming, conniving.

I rolled a tightly coiled half sheet of blank writing paper up and used string from my sock to construct a handmade barrel for the ink pen-filler they issued me. I made a ninety-day calendar and stuck it to my wall using soap as glue. On the calendar I formulated a workout routine; arms and legs on Monday, Wednesday, Friday, and chest and stomach on Tuesday, Thursday, and Saturday. Sunday was my off day. I also wrote down a few reminders: what days I showered, what days they picked up and passed out library books, and other notable benchmarks.

On my tenth day in lockup I went to classification and was told that I would have to remain in the hole until the disciplinary process regarding my mutual combat charge was adjudicated. I was cleared for Ad-Seg yard and informed I had a right to appeal the committee's action if I so chose to.

I slowly walked back to my cell feeling hella wronged, the expression on my face remaining impassive as I passed the other cells on the tier. Conversations ceased as the guard escorted me to my cell with a firm hand under my armpit and a black metal baton at the ready in his other hand. When I was four doors from my cell, out the corner of my eye, I saw a black face and the bright whites of the cell soldier's eyes as I walked by. He mumbled some unintelligible shit under his breath after I passed. I gritted my teeth and clenched my fists as I neared my door.

"Back up to the tray slot and stick your hands out, palms up." The guard's voice bellowed the clear and concise command. I did as I was told and rubbed my wrists after the tray slot slammed shut.

I looked at the calendar on the wall, and my eyes narrowed to devious slits as they zoomed in on the square indicating tomorrow's schedule: it was yard and shower day. I sat down on the edge of my bed and took a deep breath, then closed my eyes and collected my thoughts: plotting, scheming, conniving.

Early the next morning immediately following breakfast a guard walked up to my cell with a clipboard and an ink pen in his hand.

"Davis, are you going to the yard this morning?" he asked and waited with the tip of the pen lingering near the paper, awaiting my answer.

“Absolutely,” I responded in a calm tone.

“Get ready. You’ll be going out in fifteen minutes.” The guard stated as he walked away.

“Aight.” I pulled my socks up as high as they would go and laced my shoes up tight as I could, then I paced back and forth in my concrete cage, fully engaging the volcanic rage building within me. Every few minutes I’d stop and shadow box in the corner for several seconds, imagining the many different possible scenarios that could play out within the hour. “This is the type of shit you been doin’ for years Mike! No love! No mercy! Beat his bitch ass for his disrespect!” the wicked voice of unreason in my head silently prodded as I turned up in preparation for battle. Hurt people hurt people. Violence was the only way I knew how to communicate when somebody hurt my feelings, or said something I deemed to be disrespectful. It was the violent dynamic of the solitary mentality I developed from years of being locked up and isolated in 6’ x 9’ concrete cages when I acted up.

The sound of jingling keys alerted me that the po-po was coming to get me for yard. I tucked my towel under my arm and collected my breath as the guard’s key slid in and popped the tray slot open. I moved my tongue around the inside of my mouth to generate some type of moisture.

Clank!

I backed up to the door and stuck my hands out, palms up. My heart rate sped up as my chest filled with excited adrenaline when the guard opened my cell door. I learned at a young age to never underestimate my adversary and to never overestimate myself. I took deep controlled breaths as I strolled to the half-gravel half-asphalt yard with a handball court, pull-up bar station, and sink with a toilet next to it. When the officer undid my cuffs, I rolled my towel up, wrapped it around my neck and then tucked the ends of it inside my state issued t-shirt. I swiftly strolled to the far end of the yard and posted up against the handball wall, as far away from the entrance as possible.

A couple minutes later the cell soldier entered the yard and slowly backed up to the gate with his hands out, palms up, his gaze never straying from mine. The officer removed his cuffs then returned to the lockup unit to retrieve another inmate for yard. The cell soldier walked with an exaggerated limp in his stroll and his chest poked out like he was a lot bigger than he actually was.

I snuck a peek at the gun tower to see what the guard up there was doing. The guard had the Mini-14's nylon strap slung over his shoulder while he talked on the phone.

My eyes shifted back to the cell soldier who was about twenty feet away.

"Aye loc, I know you be hearin' me on the tier when I be gettin' at you! Why the fuck you ain't—"

Boop! Bop! Boop! Boop! Bop!

I didn't let him finish talking. I came off the handball wall and hit him in the face with the most violent combination of punches I could muster up. He frantically retreated while desperately trying to avoid my barrage, but I was on him without mercy. When he fell, I pounced on top of him and continued to beat on his face with my fists.

"Break it up! Break it up damn it! Stop fighting and get down!" the guard in the tower ordered as loudly as he could. I heard the piercing scream of the alarm sounding off and felt the slick blood from cell soldier's open wounds on my knuckles. A sense of calmness came over me at that moment. I got off of him after a couple more brutal punches and took a step backward.

"Get your bitch ass up and chunk 'em punk!" I shouted, bouncing on the balls of my feet in anticipation for some more squabbling. Cell soldier got up off the ground and assumed a defensive position with his hands swinging wildly in front of his face. I heard the sound of a gang of keys jingling loudly as a dozen officers responded to the alarm.

Me and cell soldier rushed each other at the same time and collided like a violent car crash in the middle of the yard.

We exchanged an intense flurry of blows for a few more seconds. I felt his fist connect to my face a couple times, but I was definitely socking him more than he was me.

"Get the fuck down! Get the fuck down!" I heard one of the responding guards yell as a powerful burst of orange pepper spray hit me square in the face. I instinctively shut my eyes and took a step back and to the left. My vision was hella cloudy, but I could still see the cell soldier through my orange-tinted eyes. He was lying on his stomach fully complying with the officer's orders. The burning effect from the toxic chemical agent on my skin and in my eyes was almost intolerable. I choked and coughed loudly as I desperately tried to catch my breath. I lay face down on the ground while my face burned like a wildfire. Long strips of snot dripped from my nose as I grit my teeth and fought to "man up."

They took the cell soldier off the yard first. After what felt like half an hour the guards took their time and walked me inside to rinse off in one of the showers.

Later that night ...

"Davis, you eatin' dinner?" the guard asked after opening my tray slot.

"Yup," I told him and took my tray. I sat the tray on the desk and prepared to dig into the spaghetti with meatballs, green beans, and a slice of garlic bread.

When the guard moved four doors down, he banged his heavy brass key on the door to get the cell soldier's attention.

"Aye Jackson, are you eating dinner?" he asked. A couple of seconds of silence passed. "Turn your light on then!" the guard instructed. Another couple of seconds passed before the tray slot opened. "Damn Jackson, you got the shit beat out of you!" the guard exclaimed loudly with a snicker that caused a few others to laugh. The tray slot slammed shut and for the first time since I'd been in the hole the cell soldier didn't have anything to say.

A sly smile creased my lips and I privately allowed myself to have a good chuckle for the first time since going to the hole. "I bet his bitch ass don't talk tough no more!" I quietly muttered as I scooped up a meatball with my plastic spork and guided it toward my smiling mouth.

Reflection

This story is based on real events. Unfortunately, it's also a reflection of the savage "solitary mentality" I had when I was a lost soul in a cold world struggling to find myself. Having been severely victimized as a child, the complex trauma I suffered led to me developing a warped belief system growing up. At that particular time in my life, I was in the middle of serving twenty-eight years in prison. I was in a dog-eat-dog world, and as far as I was concerned, I refused to be the dog that got ate. I wasn't going to be anybody's food anymore.

Many of us went to prison as predators, and then we were forced to take on stronger predatory mindsets because we secretly feared becoming the prey. When locked in a 6' x 9' concrete cage, isolated from the rest of the world, this savage-like mindset only deepens. You start developing ways to cope and deal with your situation, and if your thinking is already fucked up, then you'll probably develop fucked-up coping methods in order to survive.

My "solitary mentality" was deeply rooted due to the very damaging seeds that had been planted in my head and heart at a very young age when my stepfather placed me behind a refrigerator as a way of punishment. Every time I ever got locked up in isolation, which was countless times, I unconsciously went back to that dark place, and nothing good ever came from it. In fact, I became worse; my behavior became worse. My life became worse.

I don't think parents who beat their children realize the damaging life lessons they are teaching when they violently traumatize and abuse their kids. I know that for me, and countless other *damaged children* whose paths I crossed throughout my thirty-five plus years of incarceration, one of the most destructive commonalities was that our parents taught us that when we are angered or offended, violence is an acceptable way to communicate. It was a life lesson we all took to the streets when we were old enough to do so.

A young child being beaten doesn't intellectualize those beatings with an adult's rationalization. No, they immaturely process it like a child does: *I made mommy or daddy mad, then mommy or daddy got a weapon and beat me with a weapon. I disappointed mommy or daddy, and then mommy or daddy slapped, hit, or beat me. I said something that mommy or daddy didn't like, and I got punished violently for it.* When this behavior is repeated by parents time and time again, the thought process of the child is continuously being reinforced over and over again. By the time the child is a teenager/young adult, the damage to the psyche is so deep and injurious, and the dysfunctional point of view so distorted that it becomes nearly impossible for them to recover from the damage that had been done, and the community now becomes the victim, and the cycle continues.

A Parting Thought

Community Control

Community: *a body of people living in the same place under the same laws. 2. Society at large. 3. Joint ownership. 4. Similarity, likeness.*

Control: *to exercise restraint or directing influence over: Regulate. 2. Dominate, Rule*

Initially, when I was asked to write a piece about "Community Control" I was at a loss. I was at a loss because it was a topic I had never before discussed on an intellectual level. Before offering my opinion on a subject, I first try to familiarize myself with the issue, and then give it much contemplation and serious consideration before presenting my perspective. In this case, I offer *my* rather unique point of view concerning the matter. With that said, this is my take on "Community Control."

Having been incarcerated for well over twenty-eight years (thirty-five if I include the seven years I spent in the California Youth Authority), I feel like the only community that I've been a part of long enough to offer any knowledgeable viewpoint on is the penal system in which I have been imprisoned for most of my life. And I assure you, in every prison, in every facility, and on every yard that I've ever been on, there exists a *community*. Within that *community* a particular type of *control* is ever-present and on blatant display.

Much like the free world, the prison community is a collection of segregated and fractured factions divided by race, rank, and religion. These many different divisions are almost always under the direct control, or influence, of an unwritten set of rules that must strictly be adhered to, a "penitentiary protocol" of sorts. Any violation of these said rules, real or perceived, will almost certainly yield penalties, punishments ranging anywhere from verbal chastisement to beatings or a violent death if the act is too egregious.

The politics within this *community* are mostly governed by egocentric, anti-social, ignorant individuals with deficient leadership qualities and inadequate communication skills, dictators who dominate in a predator versus prey subculture where fear ultimately rules the hearts of men. This community I speak of, or this savage world which I write about, is home to over two million human beings, all of whom give way to animalistic characteristics in order to endure in an environment where the strong survive and the weak get eaten alive. I'm talking about the evilly constructed American Prison Industrial Complex.

Environmental influences often times determine which particular "roles" the *citizens* within the *community* play. For instance, the gang members mimic the pack animals that move with a mob-like mentality, both for protection and as a show of strength and power to the adversary. They are the wolves, the lions, the hyenas, the silverbacks, the wild dogs, and the jackals, if you will. These groups tend to operate under a criterion of hierarchy made up of well-defined pecking orders, with the more sophisticated gangs comprised of levels from generals down to foot soldiers.

Then there are the substandard types of *citizens* that populate this "animal planet," the sneaky snakes that slyly slither across ethical boundary lines with scandalous schemes stirring their spirit, and the wicked-hearted weasels with acrimonious agendas feeding their greedy needs, and the dumb, unsuspecting jackasses who can't seem to get out of their own way, even to save their own lives on occasion.

Then, of course, you have the rats, roaches and other

kinds of smutty vermin who are considered the lowest of the low, the outcasts of prison society and the unwanted scum-of-the-earth within this savage world. And lastly, there are the pigs, the overseers of this shitty, inhumane civilization. They are the armed entities charged with standing sentry over the enslaved masses of "castaway savages." These cruel-minded creatures knowingly allow this sick, sadistic subculture to exist, turning a blind eye to the rampant violence perpetrated by the predators upon the prey. They are willing witnesses to the senseless incidences of mindless violence, watching with their snouts pointed high in pomposity, as iniquitous smiles decorate their contemptuous faces, their version of controlling the uncontrollable by allowing the animals to assume control while never actually giving up any control of their own.

In my eyes, this is community control in a savage world of the forgotten. At least, it is, from my unique point of view.

My tainted temple
Was painted simple
In plain colors of trial and tribulation
But my interior design
Is one of a kind
Blessed with the fruits of righteousness
And all of its glorious manifestations

Made in the USA
Monee, IL
05 July 2020

35928531R00113